Introduction

Colour your cares away with this fabulous psychedelic and abstract art colouring book. Featuring 40 different patterns and designs that you can transform into an explosion of colour and release your inner artist.

You will notice that many of the designs within this publication contain thick lines and borders which adds to the effects of each page.

Other similar titles available from the same author:

The Instant Relaxation Colouring Book: Powerful Mystic Mandalas For Mind Body & Spirit

In The Zone: The Ultimate Stress Relief Coloring Book

<u>Why not share your completed designs?</u>

You can also share your finished designs with others on our Facebook page below. Here you will also find more FREE patterns and designs for you to colour as well.

https://www.facebook.com/Best-Adult-Coloring-Books-1497039227284351/

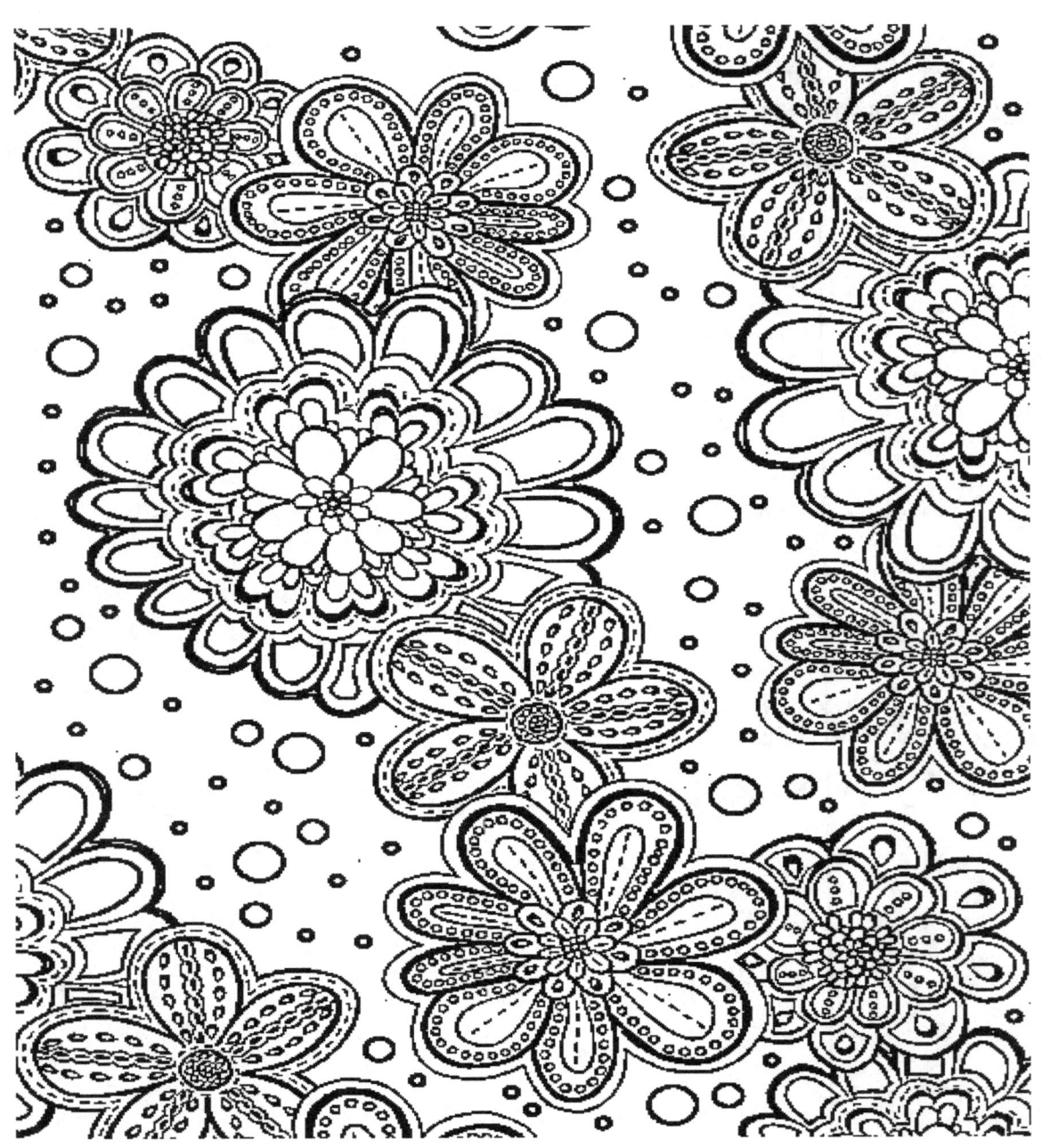

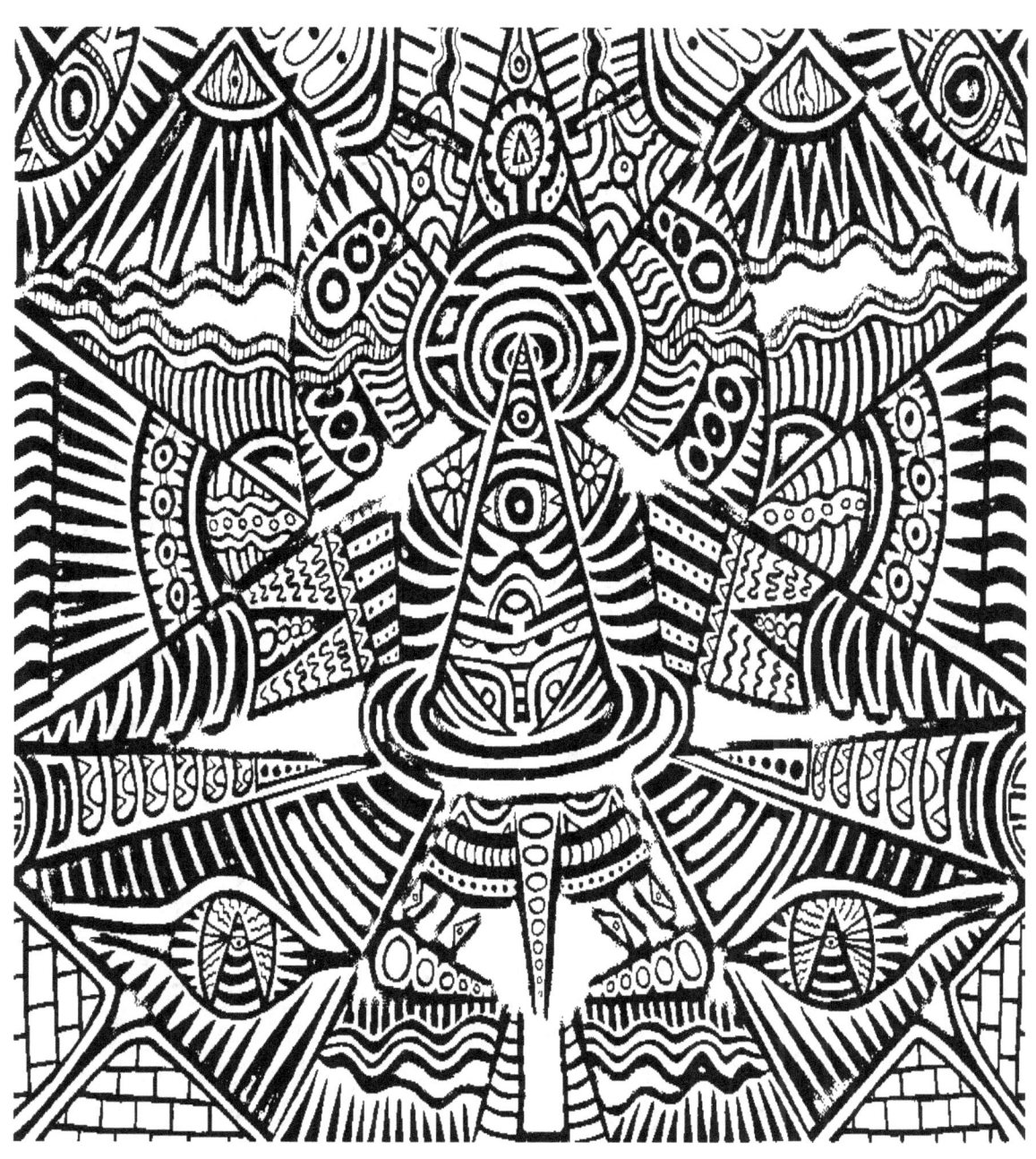

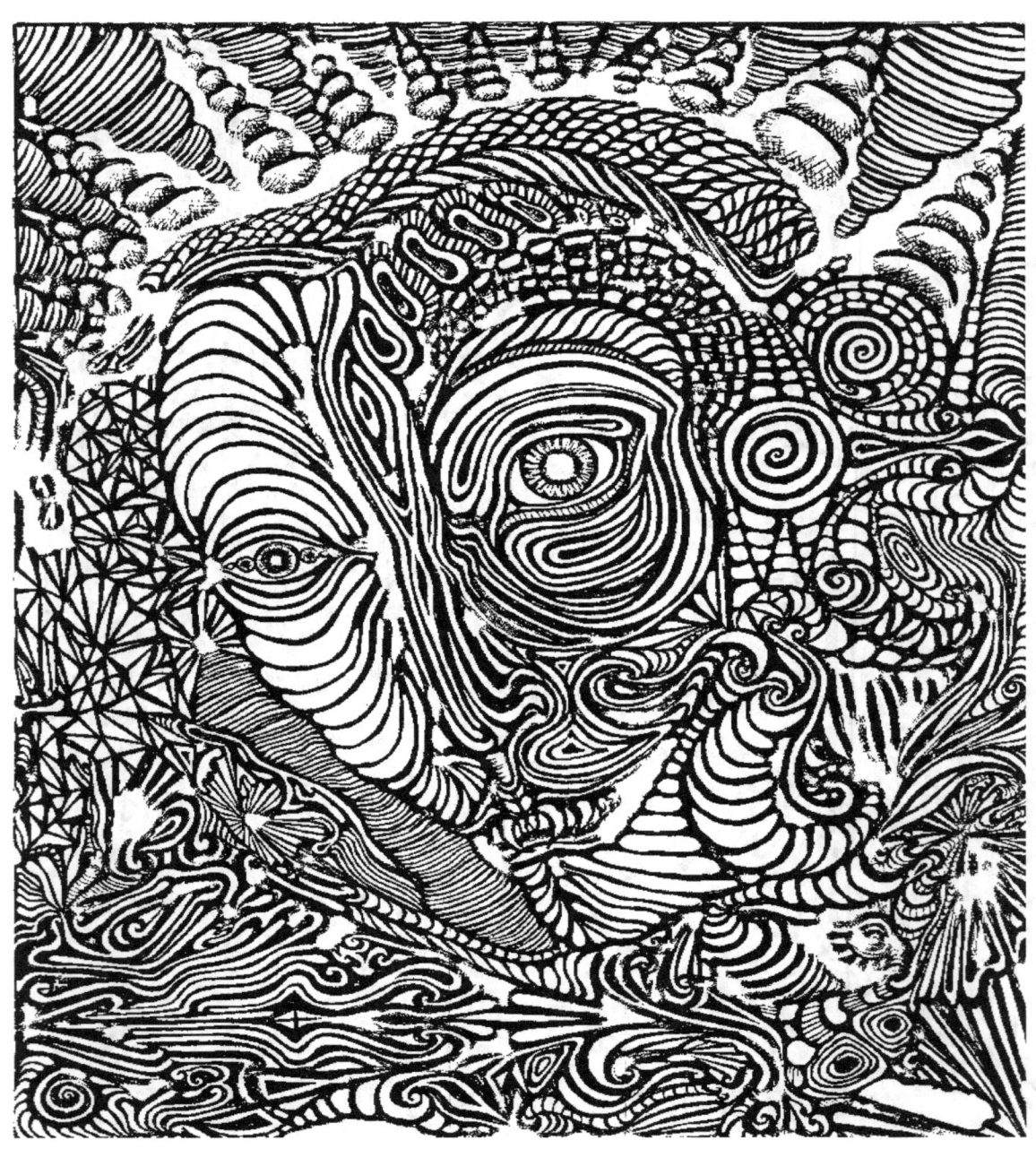

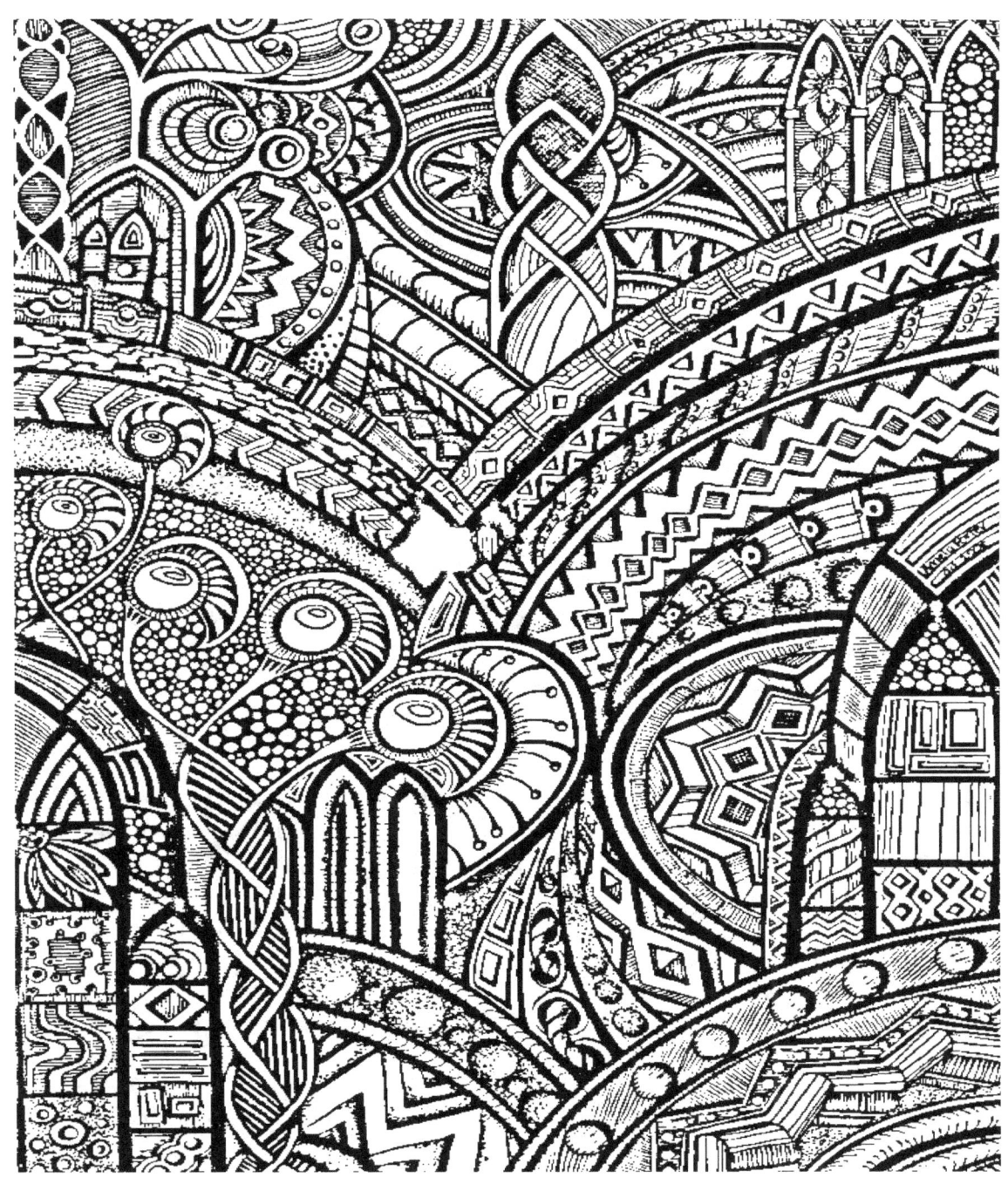

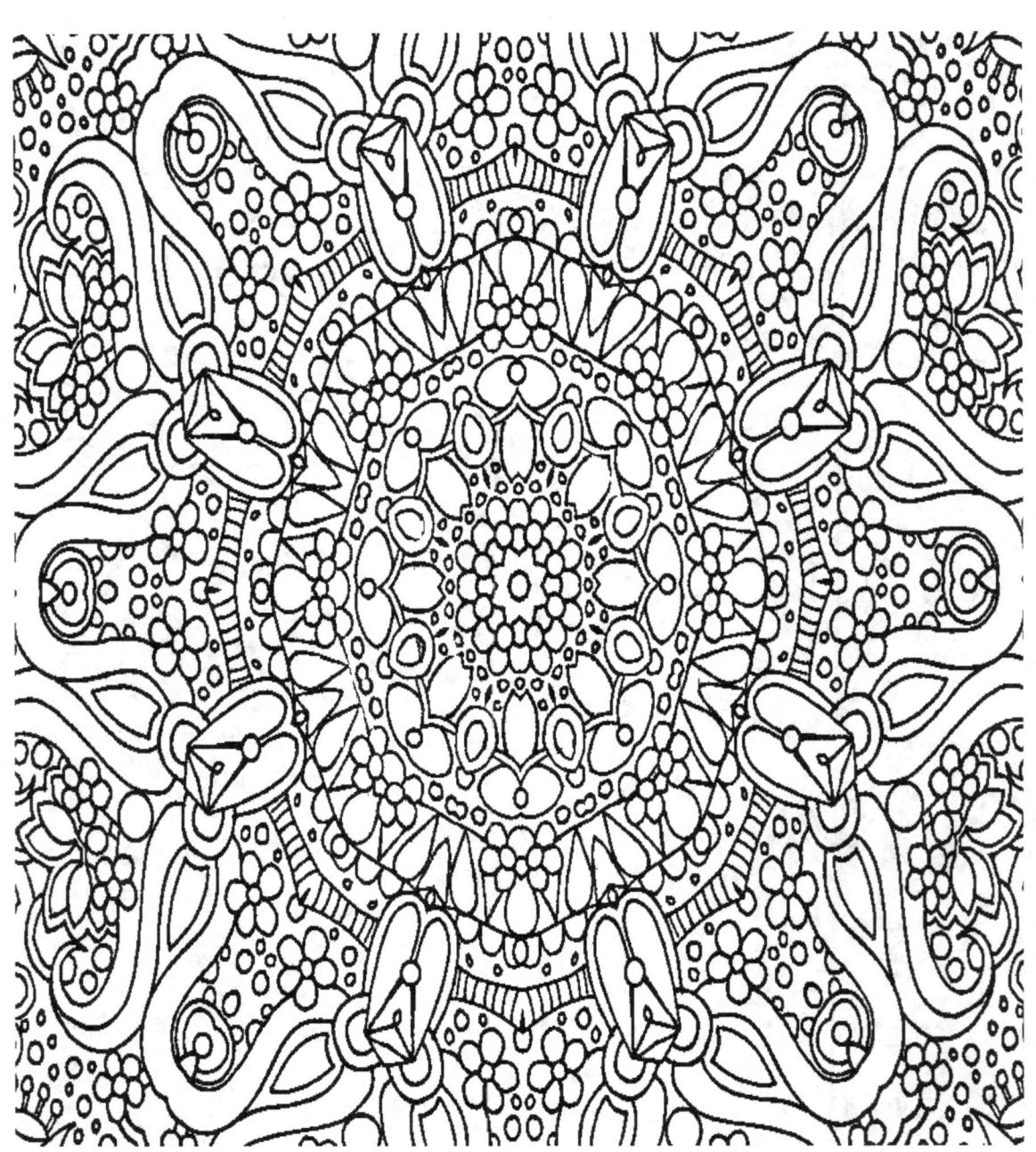

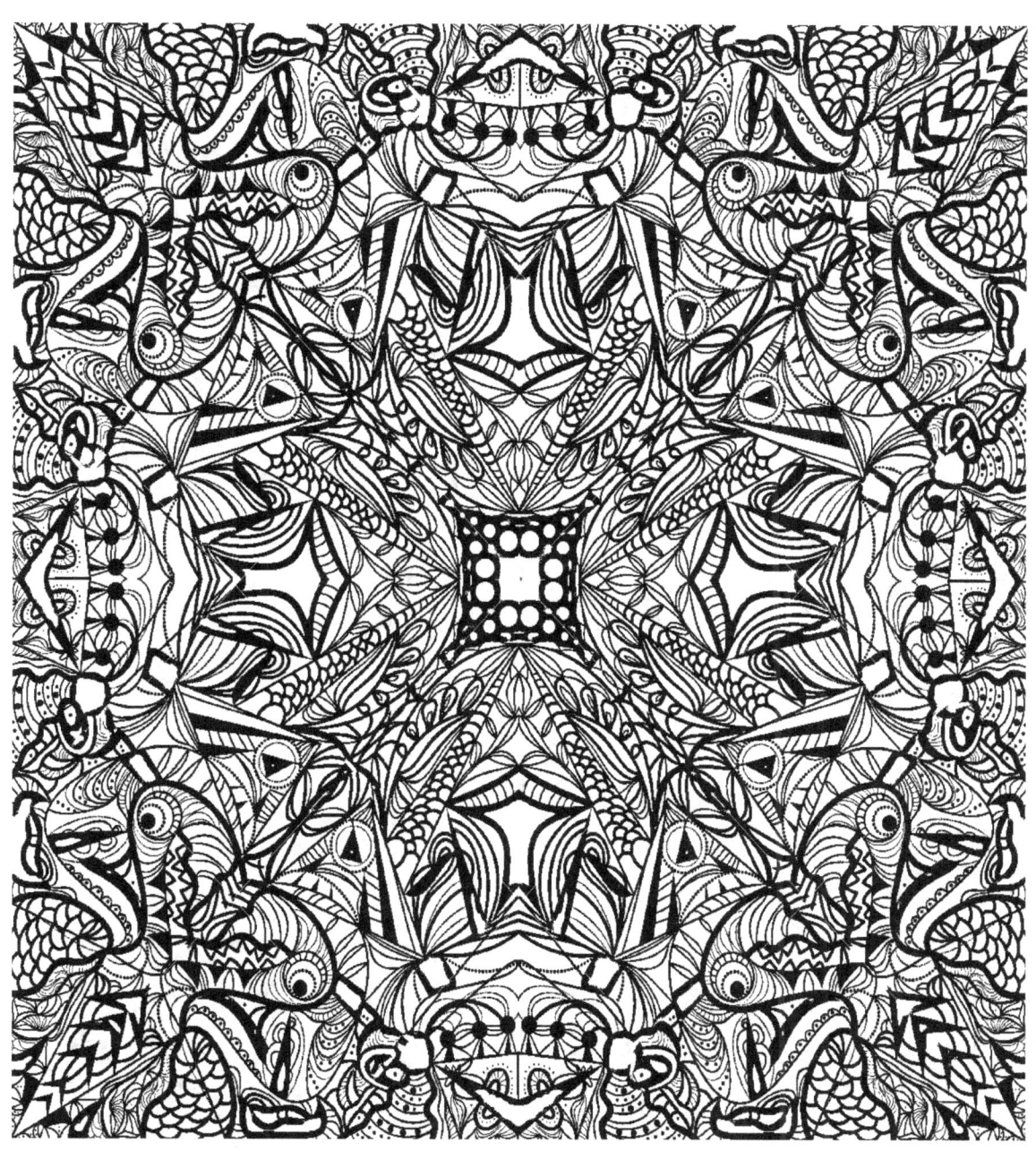

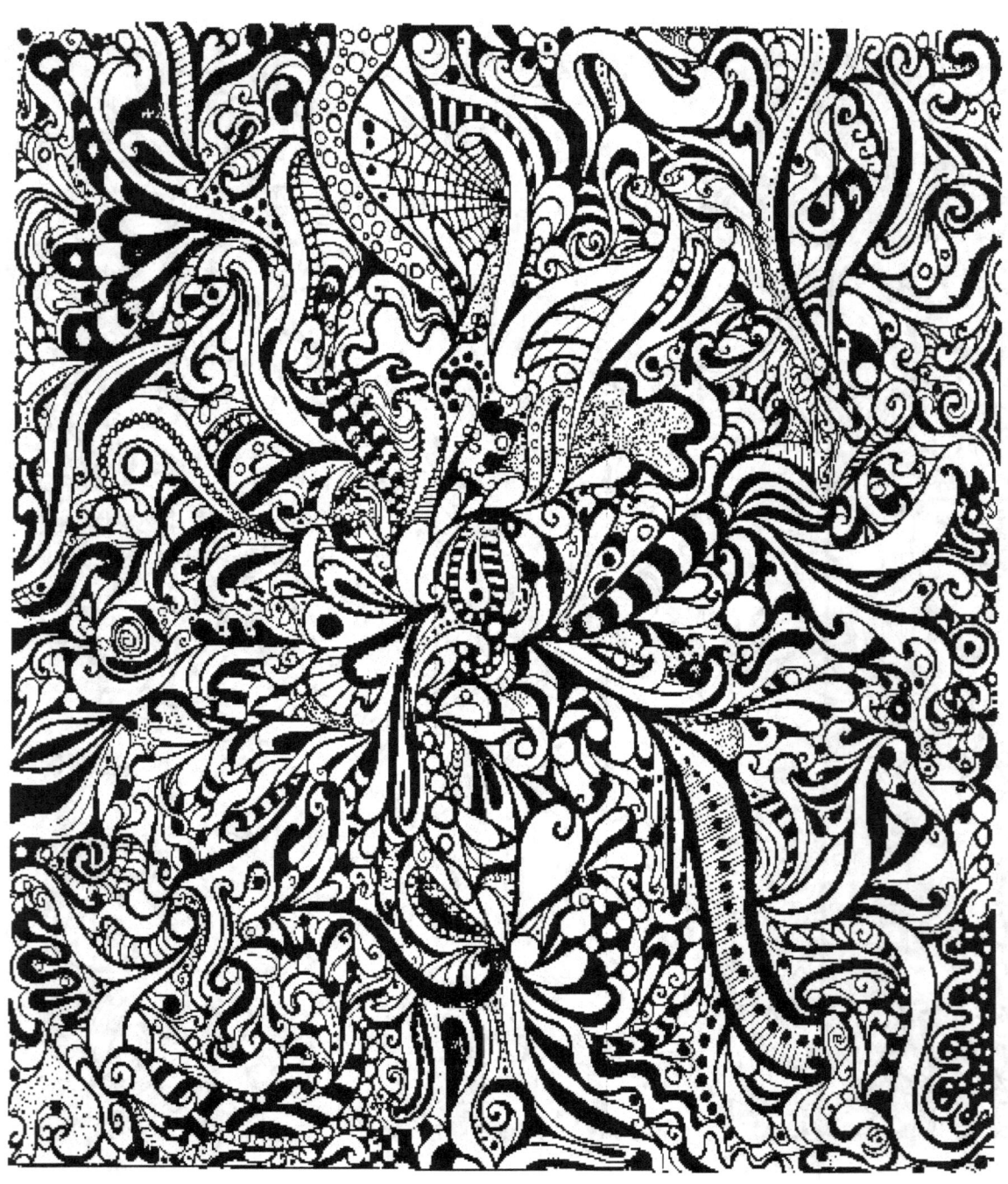

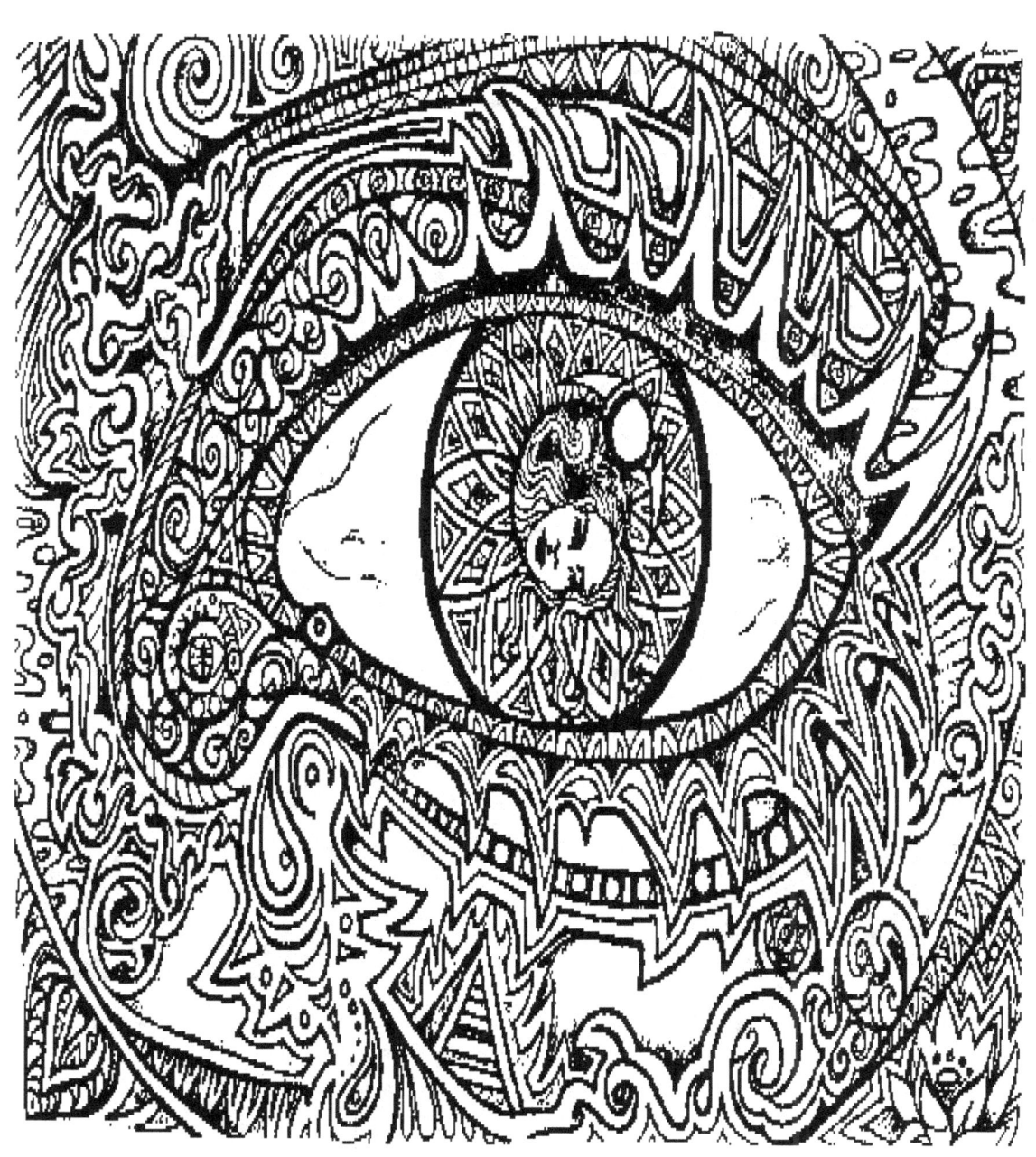

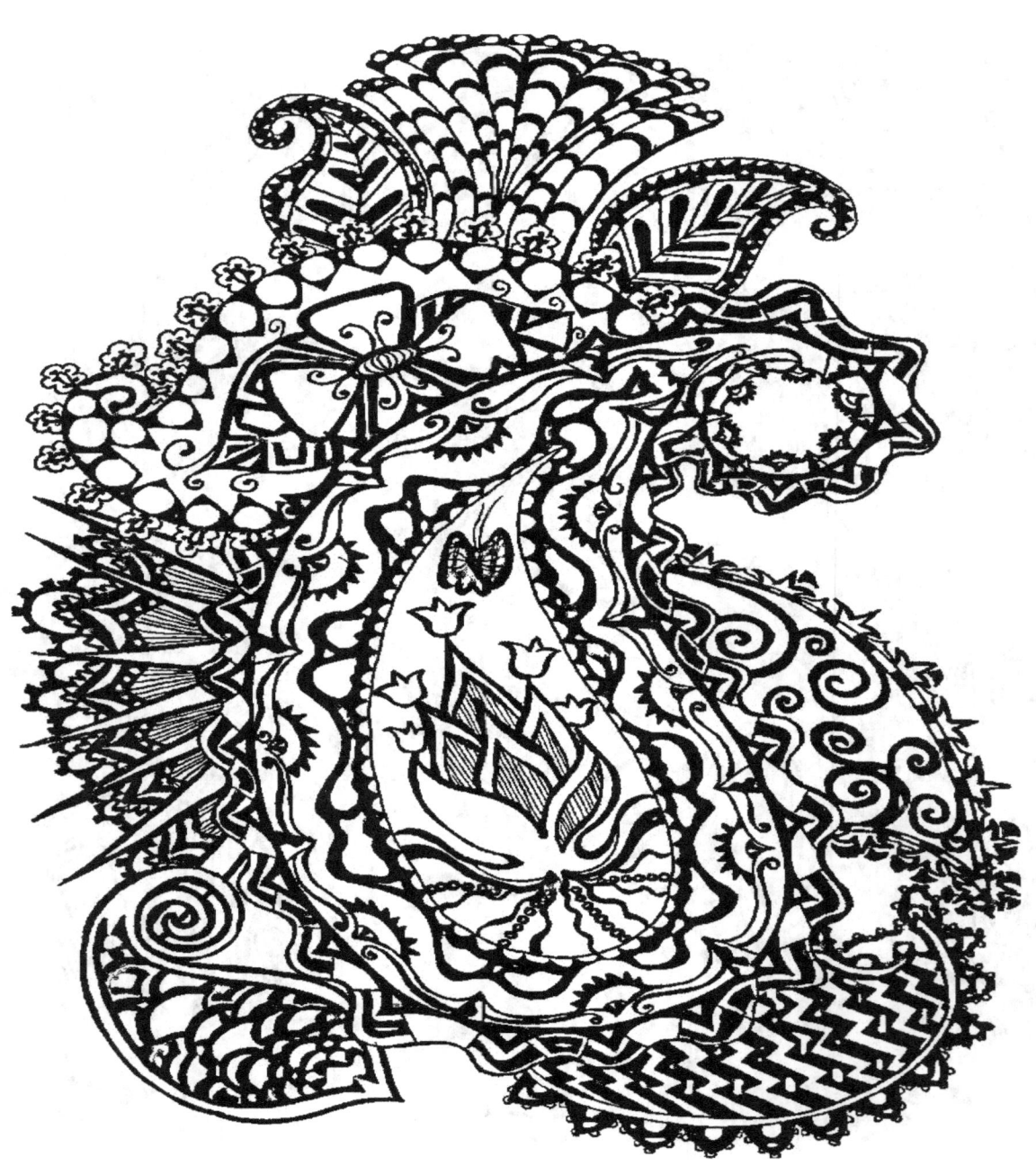

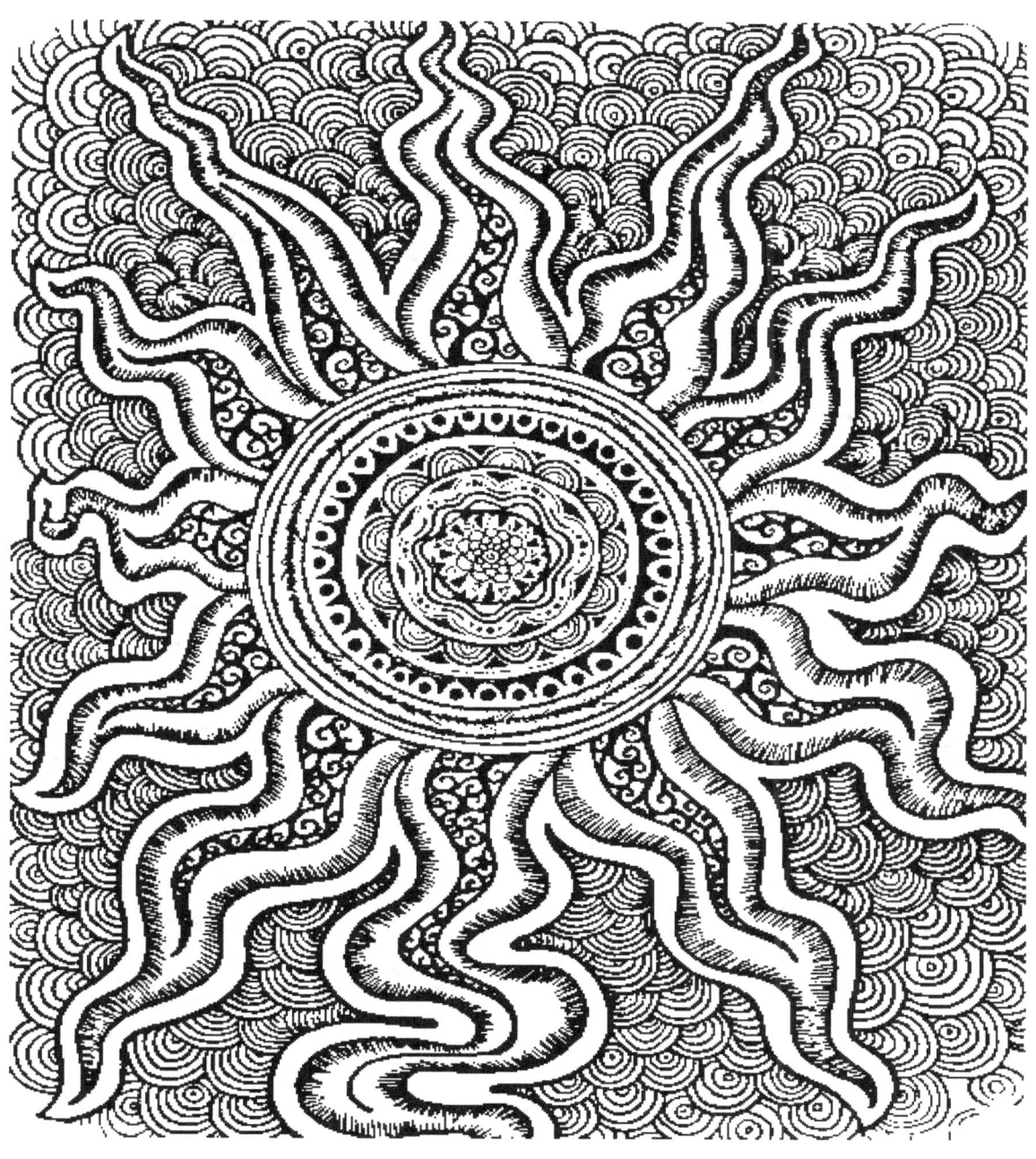

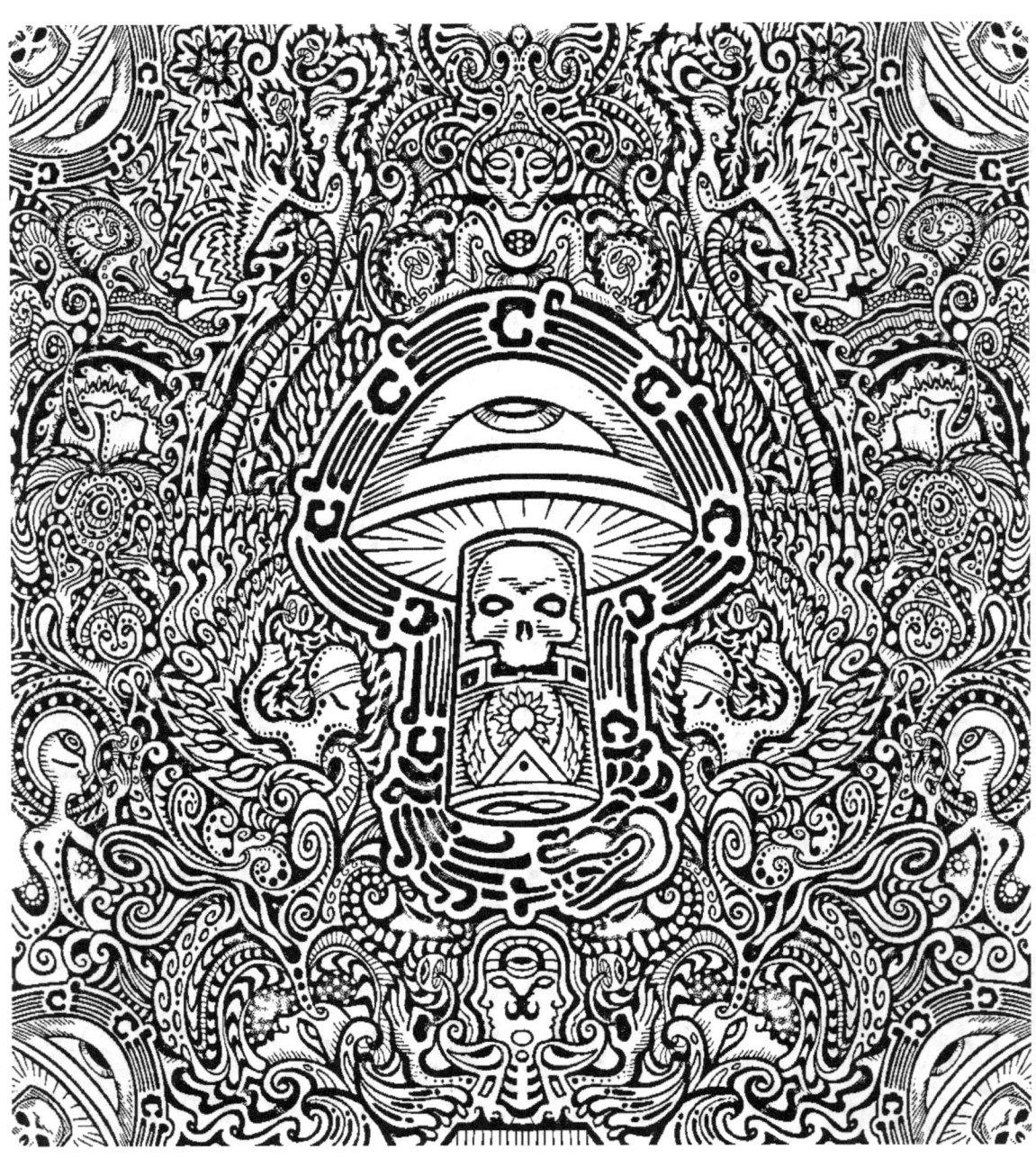

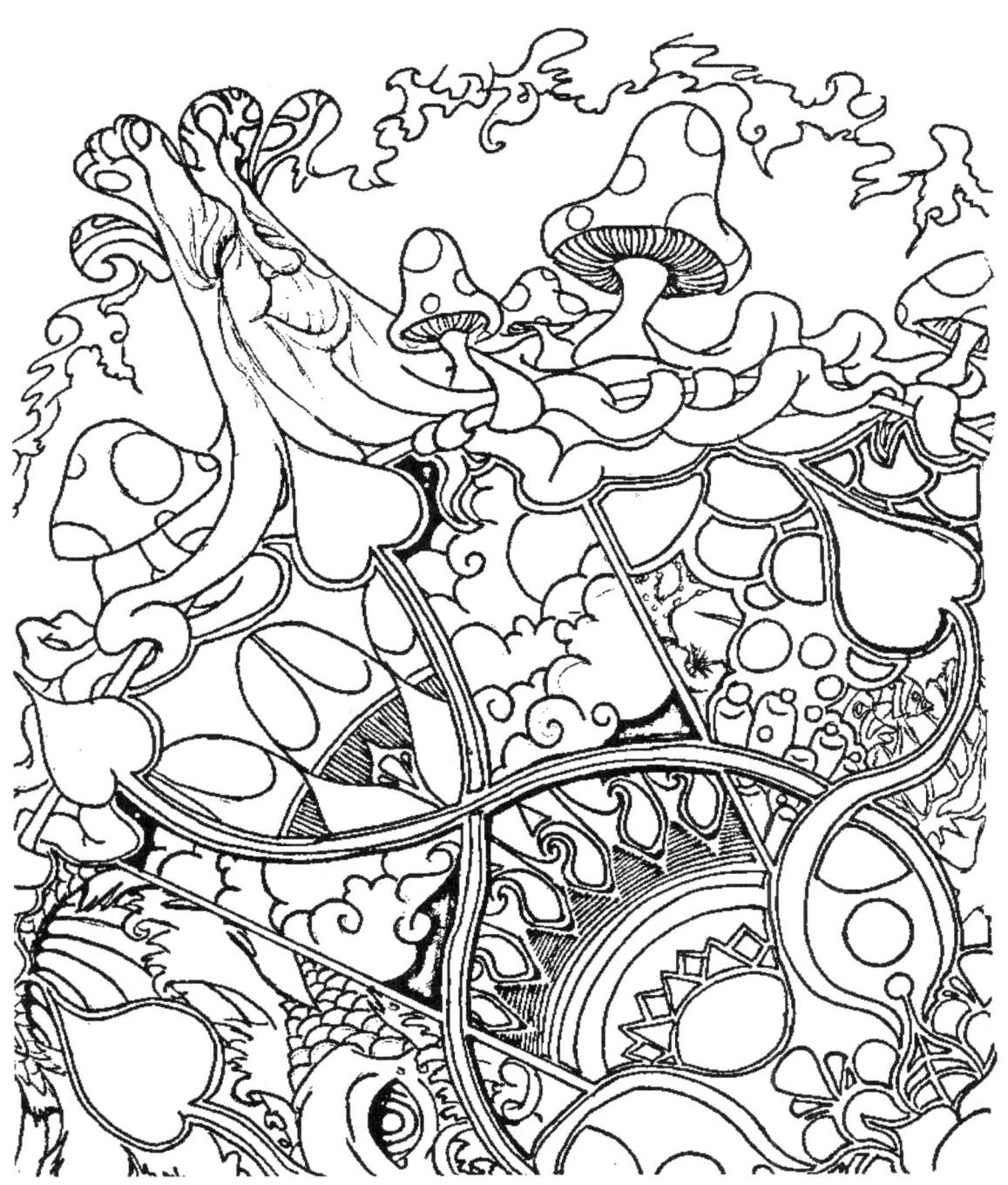

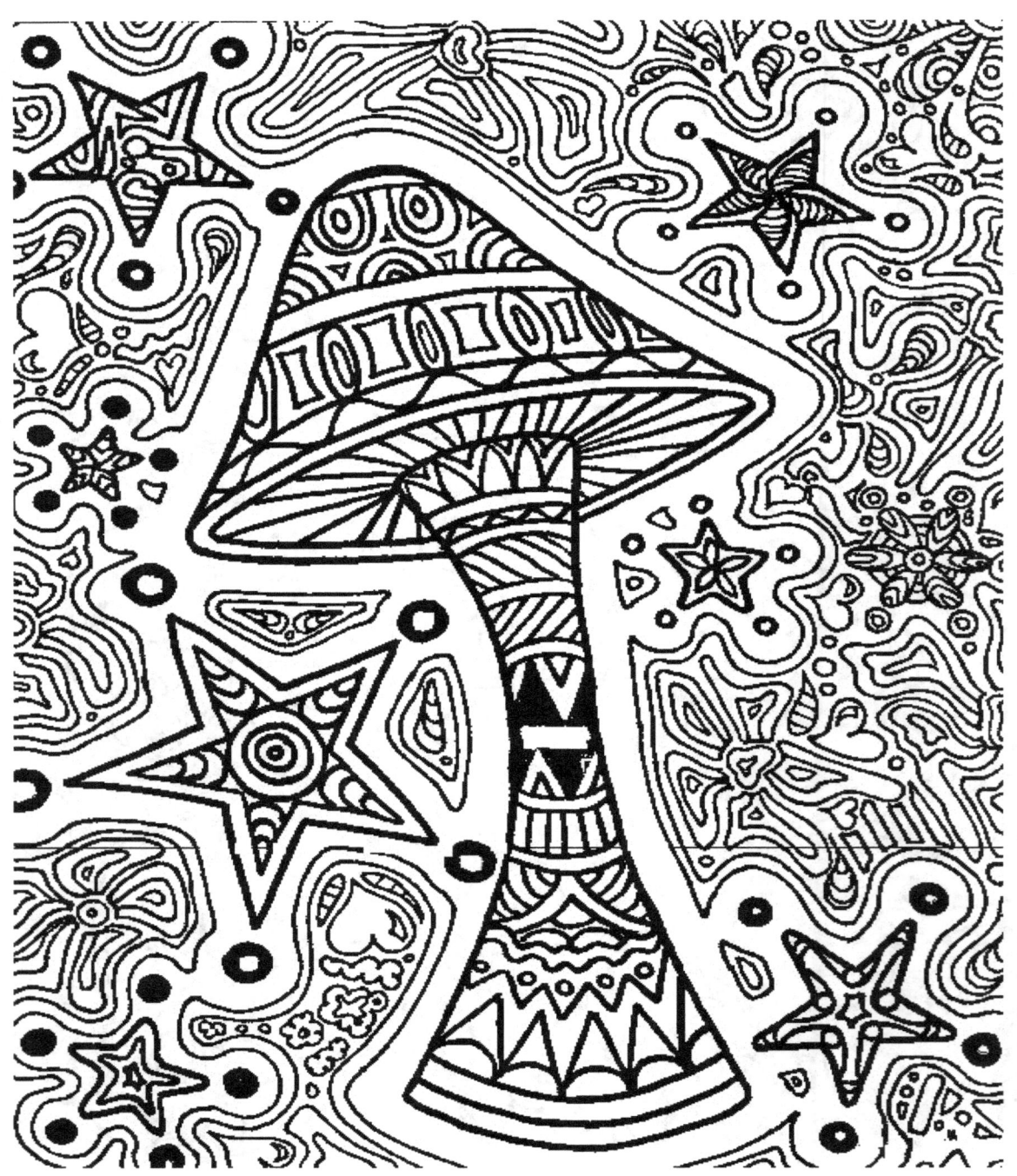

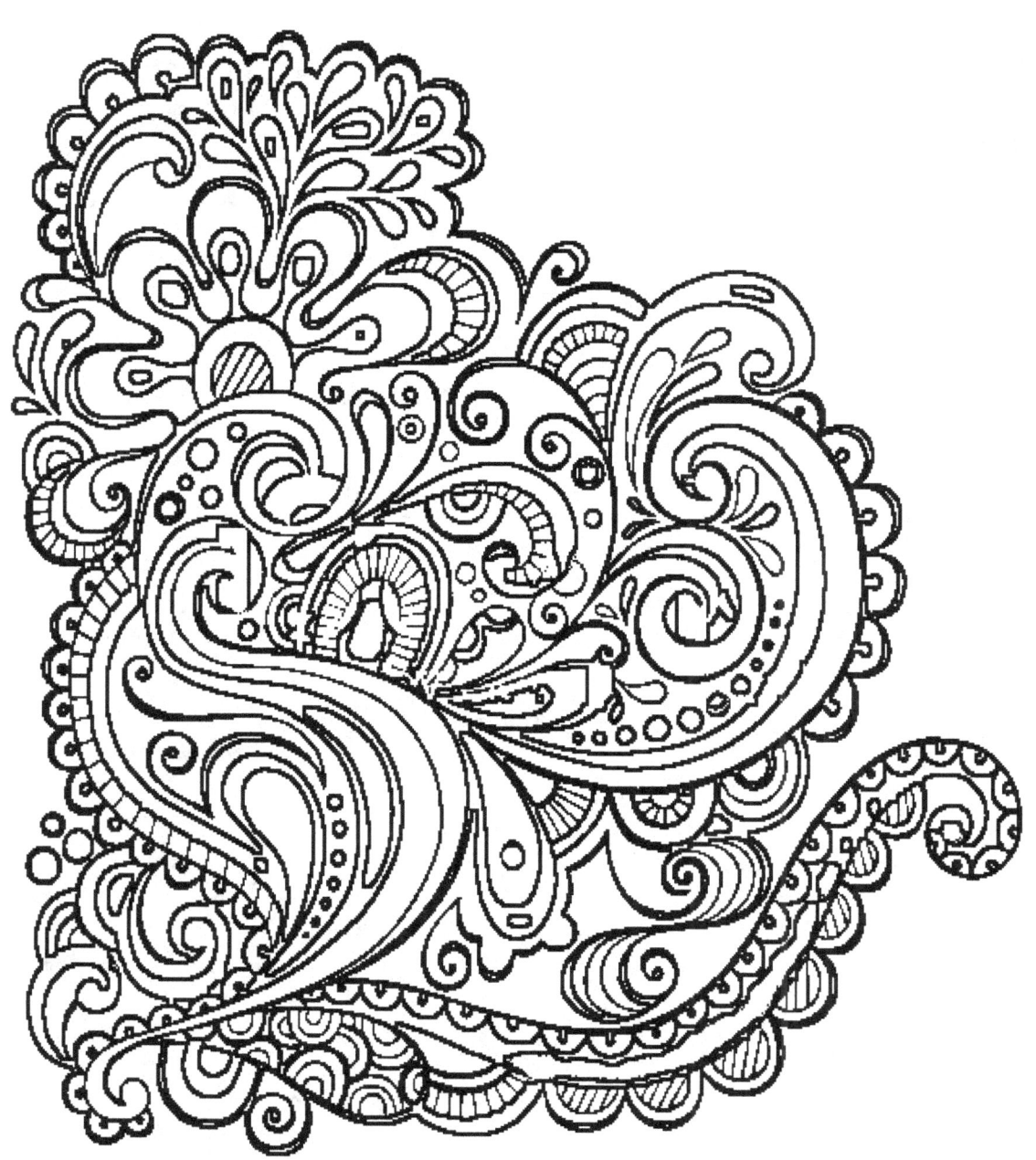

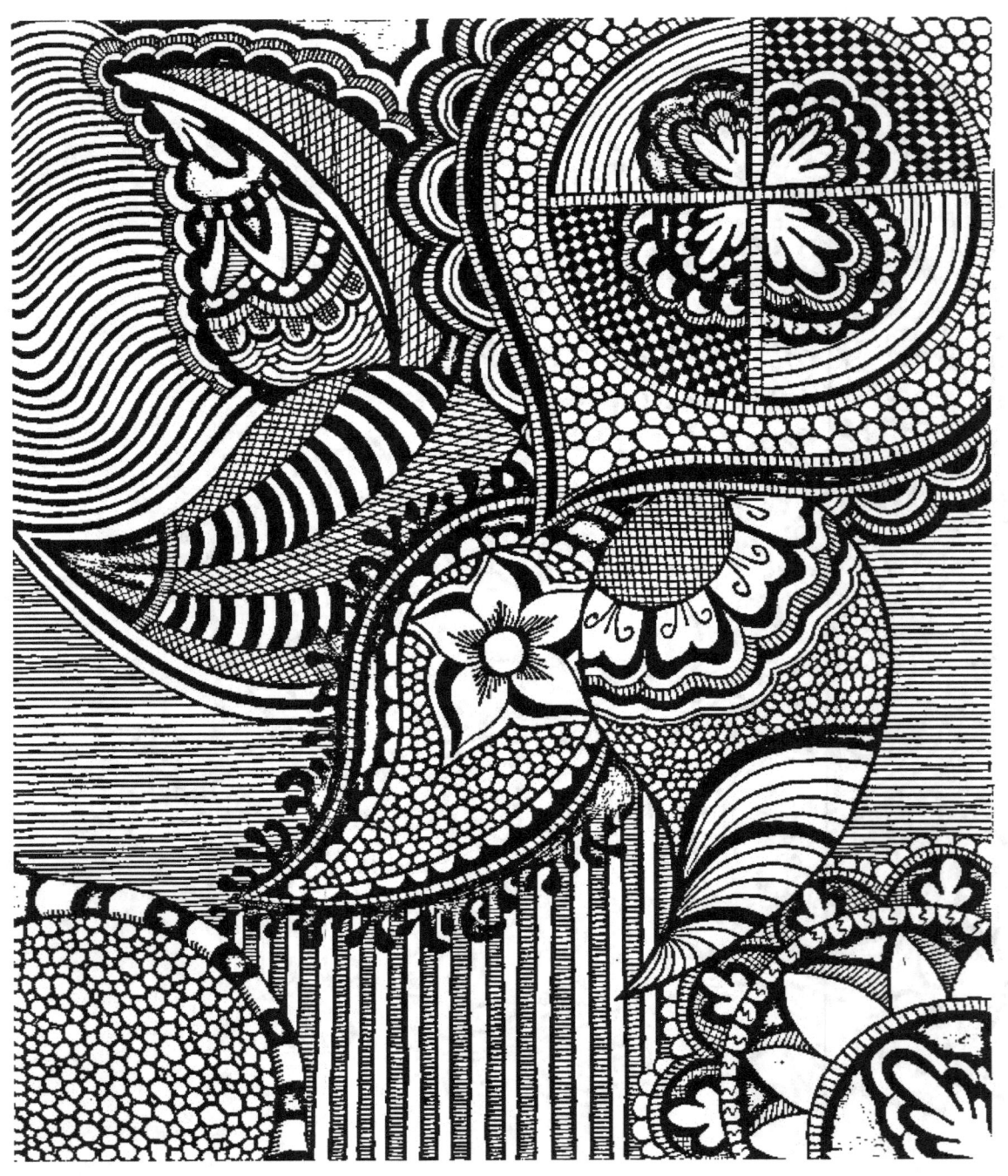

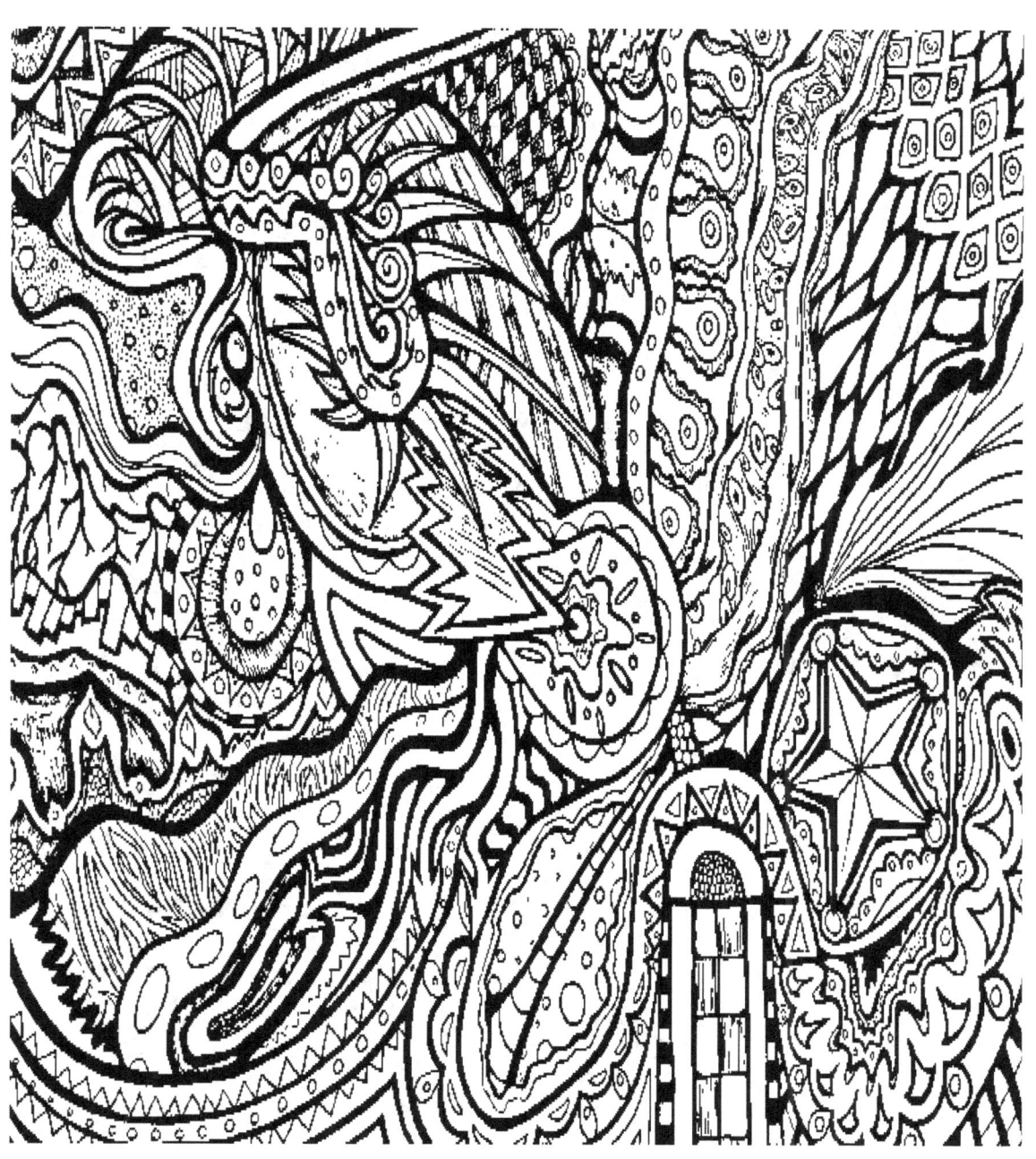

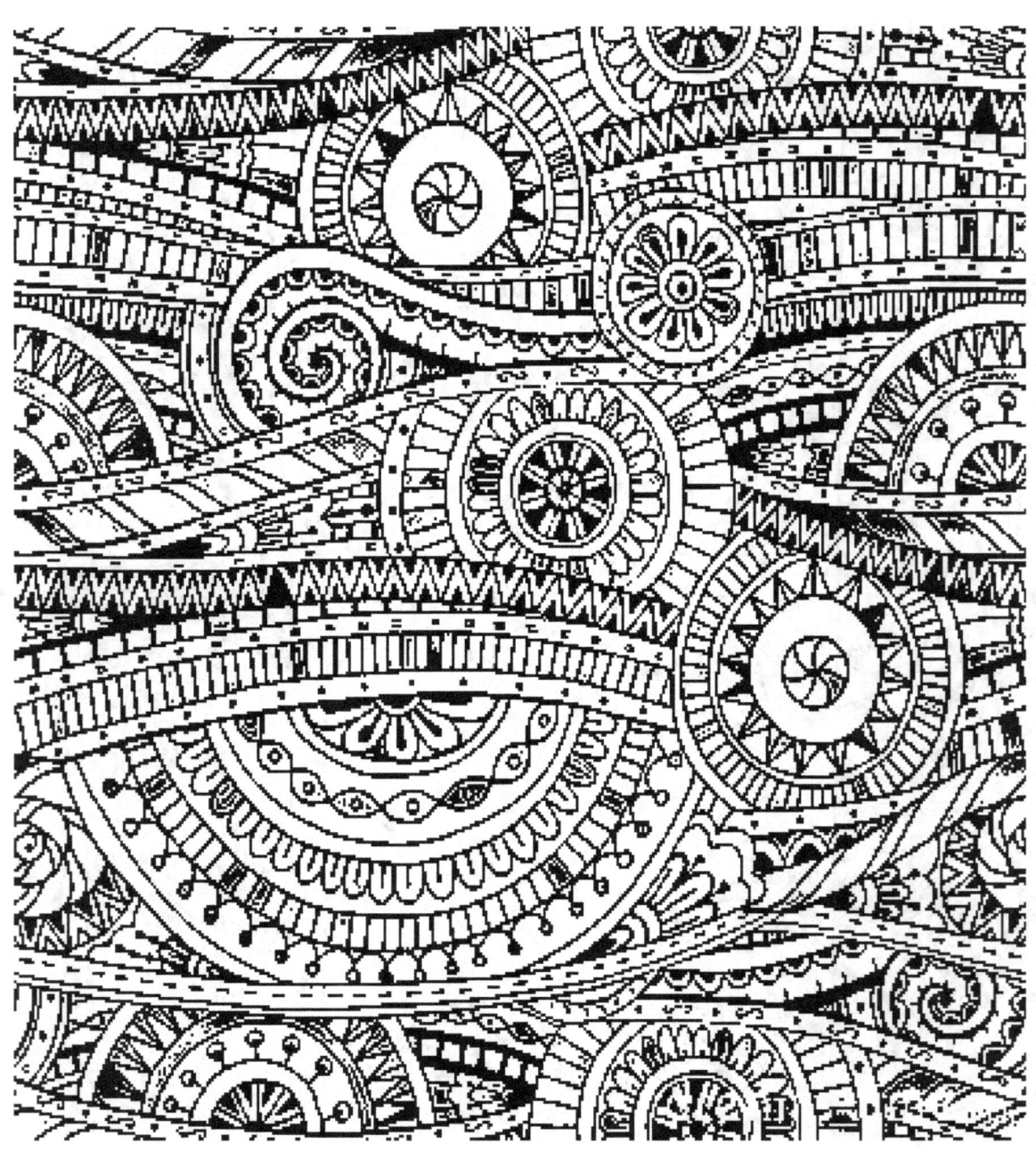

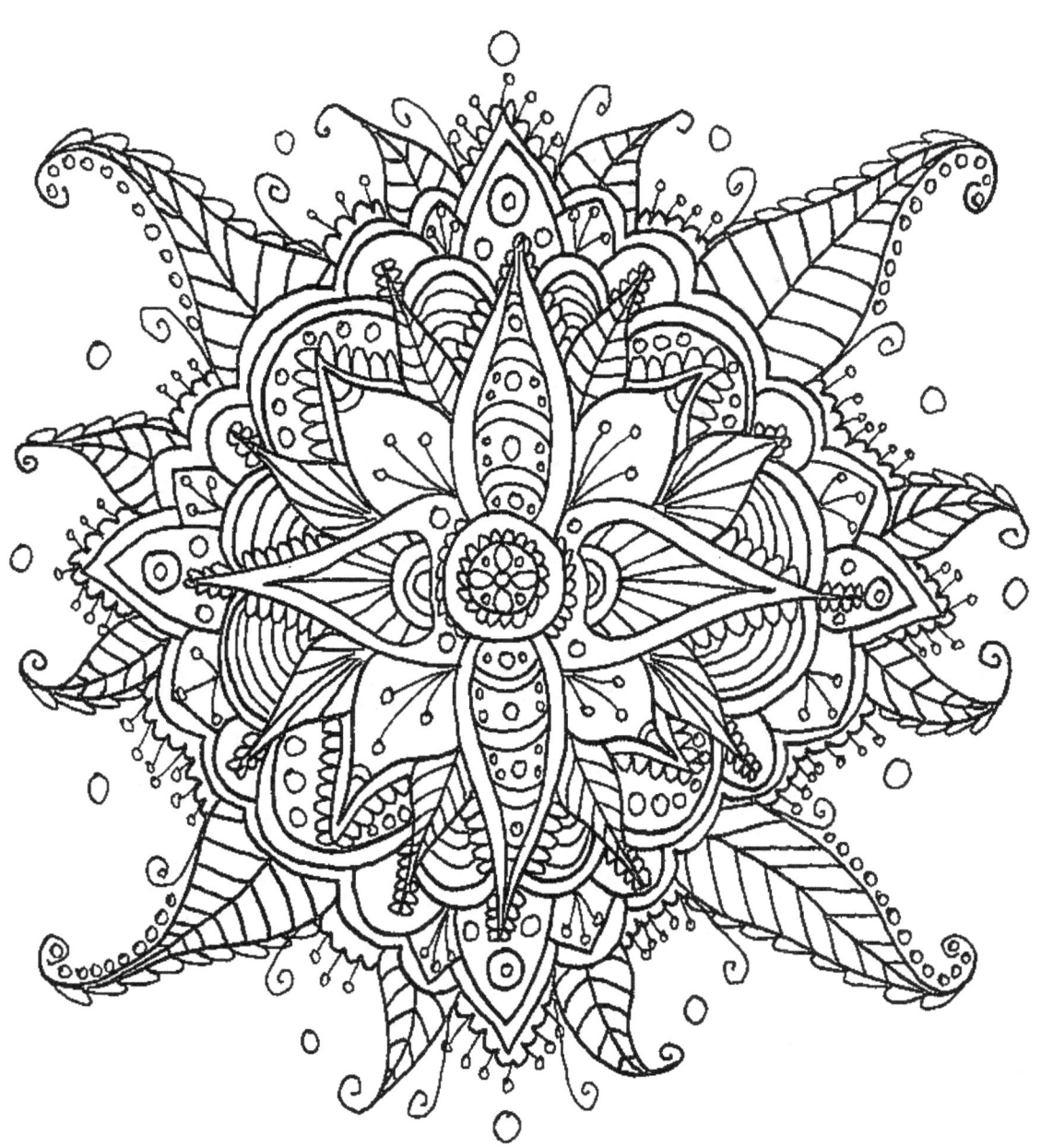

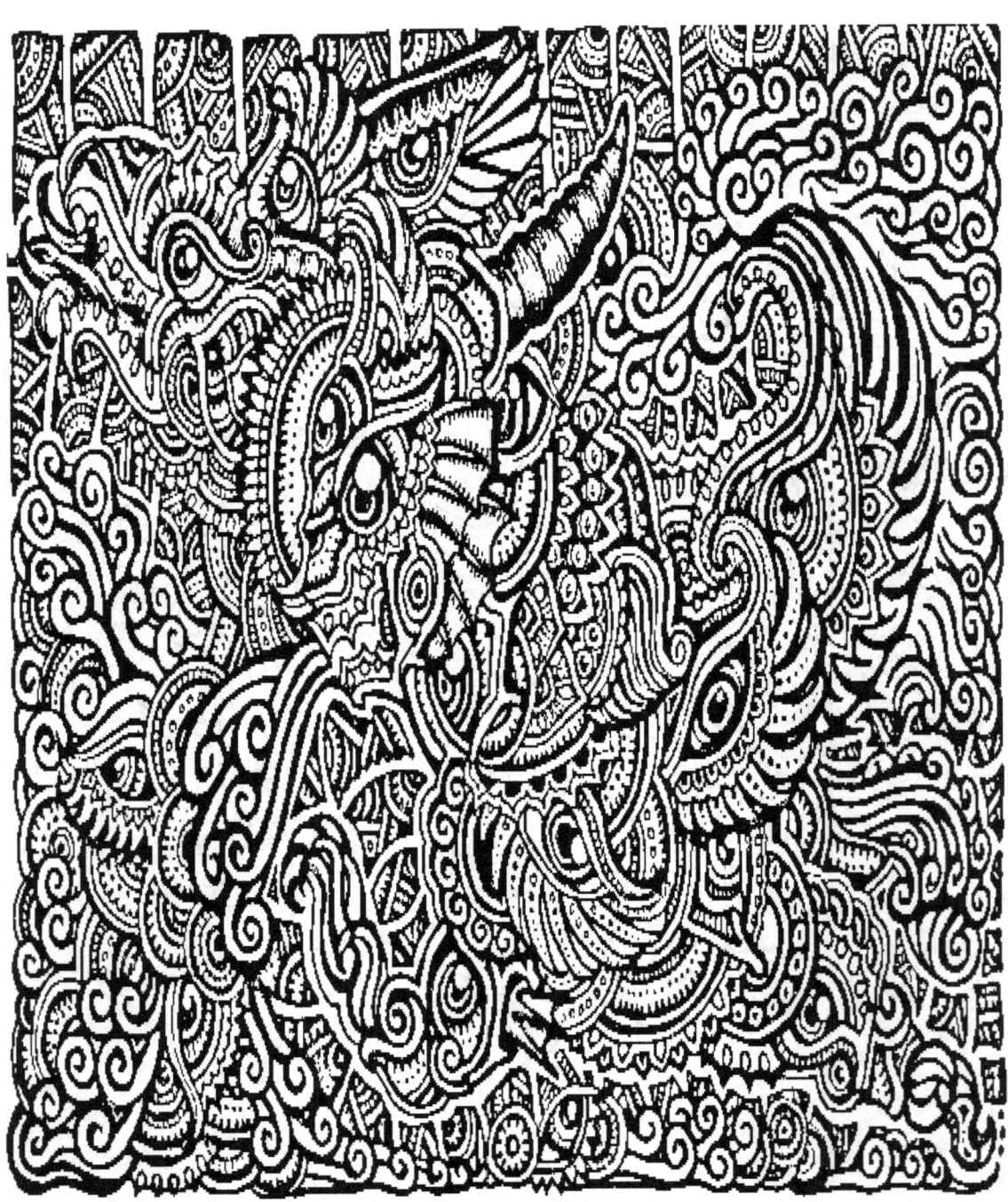

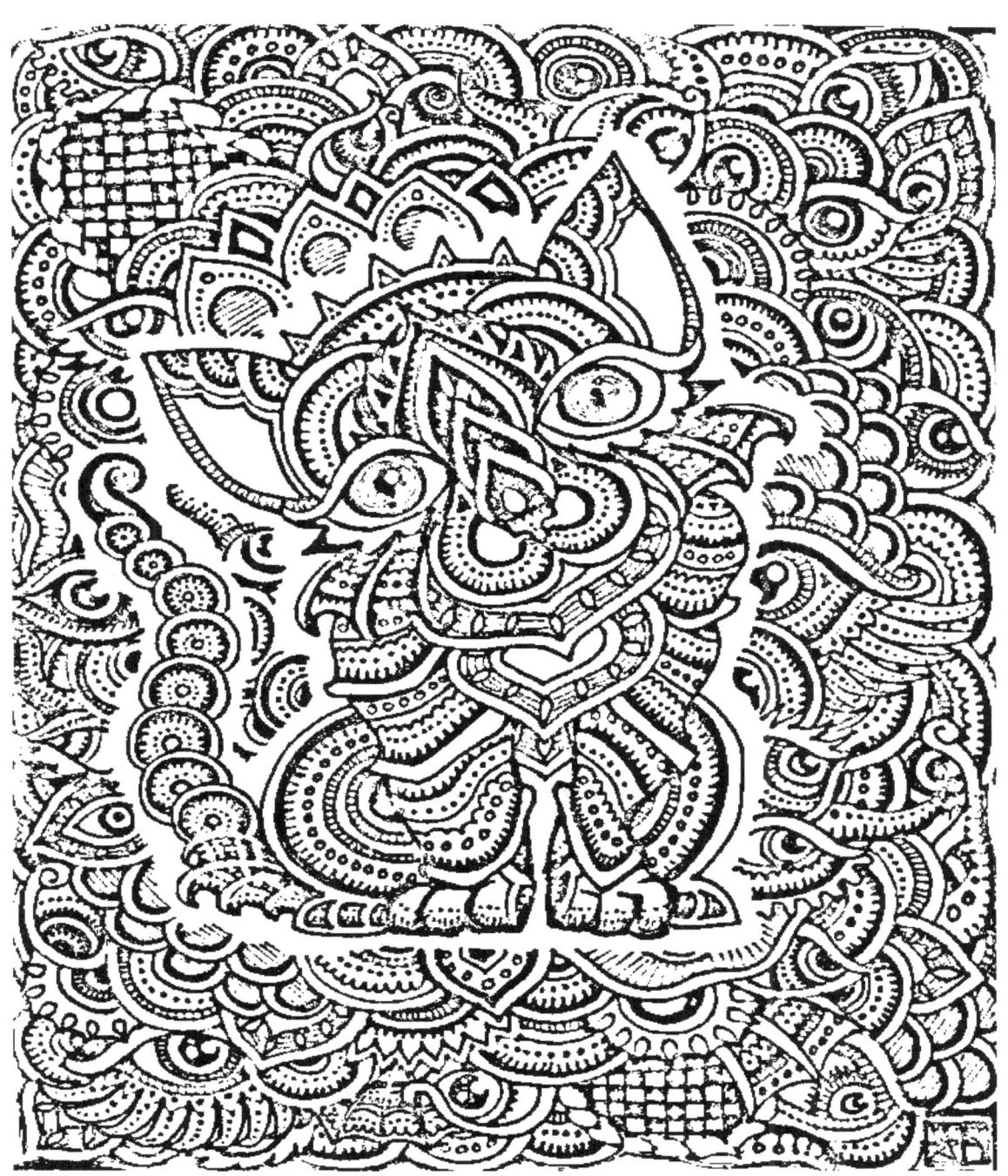

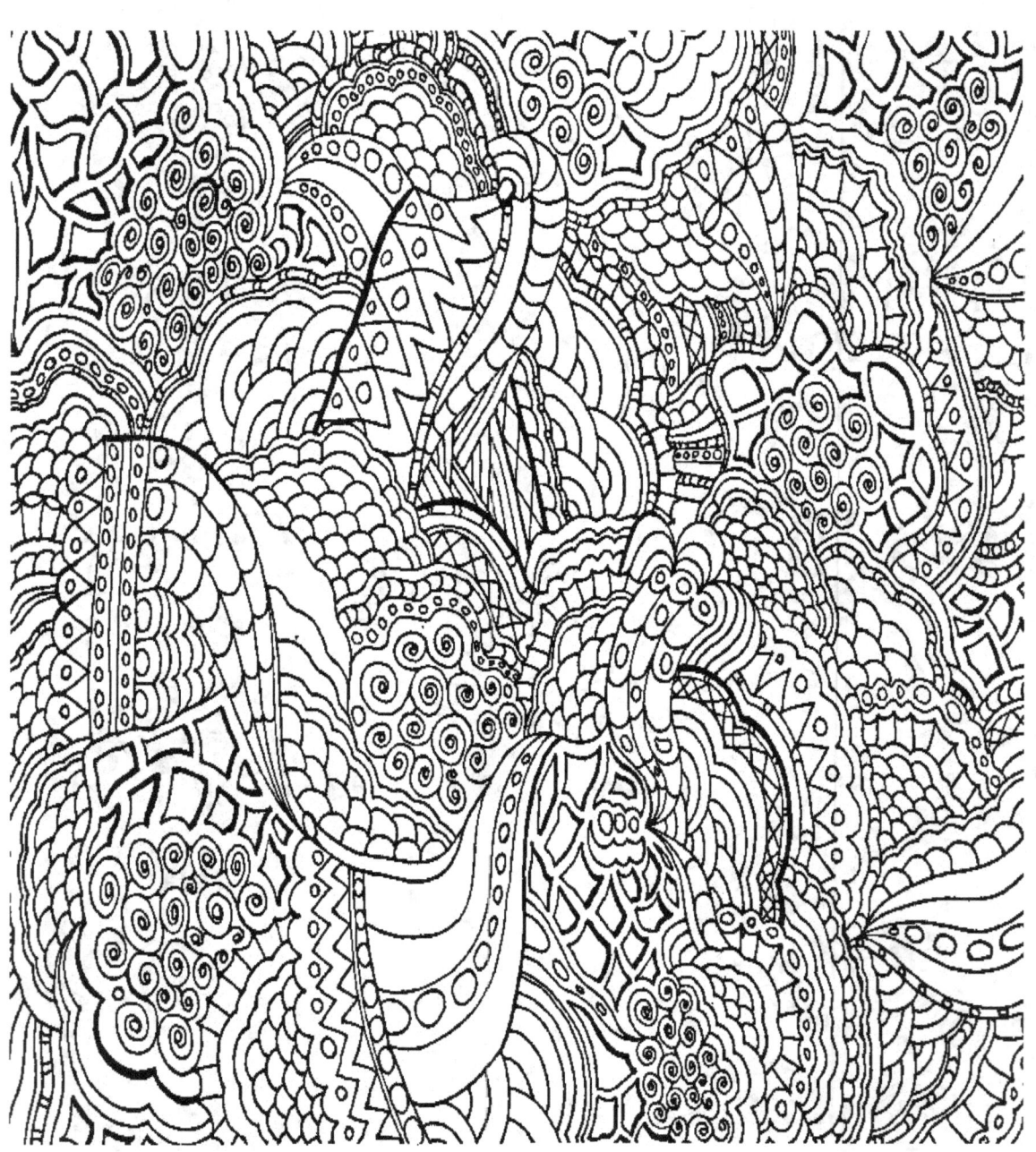

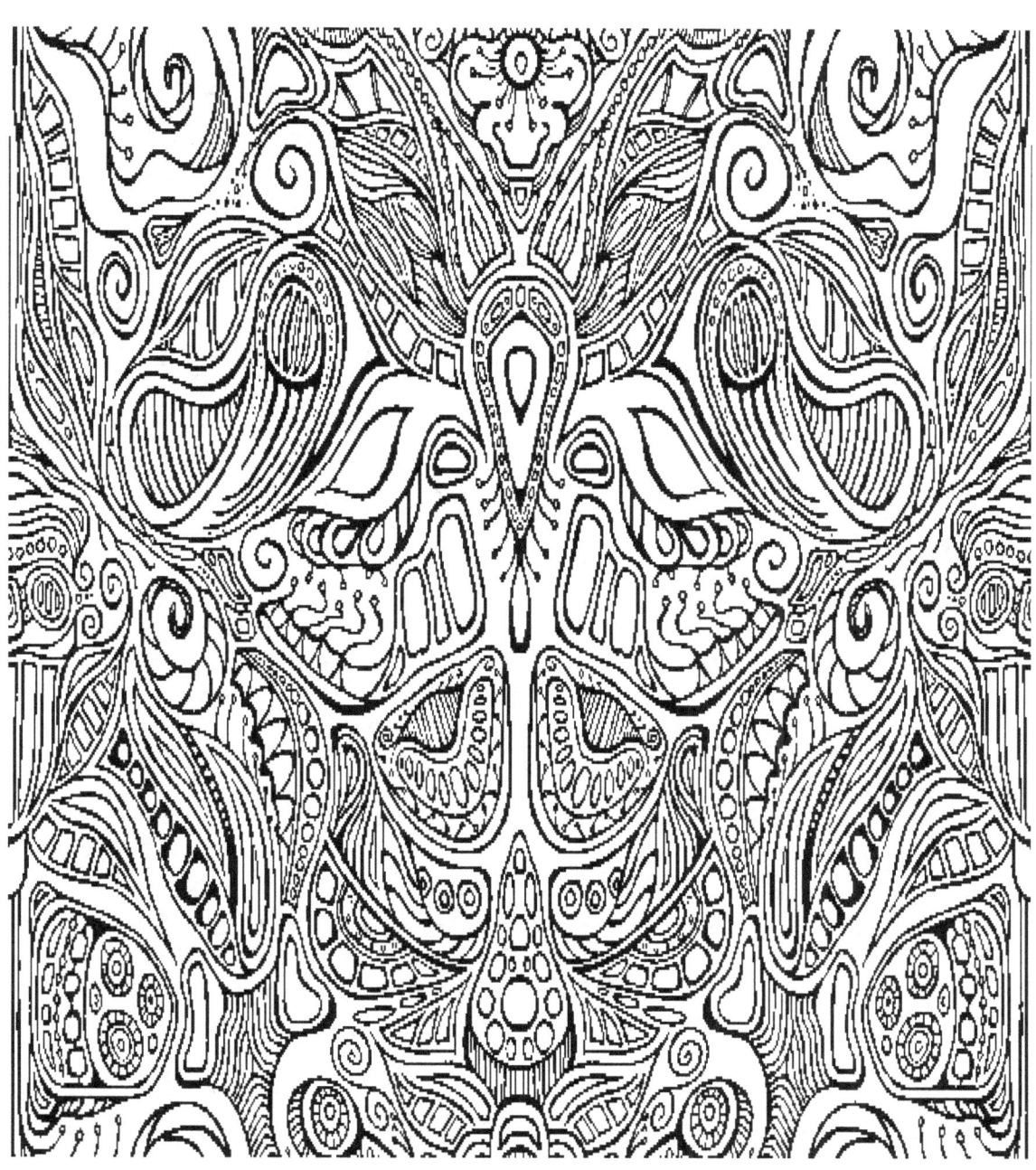

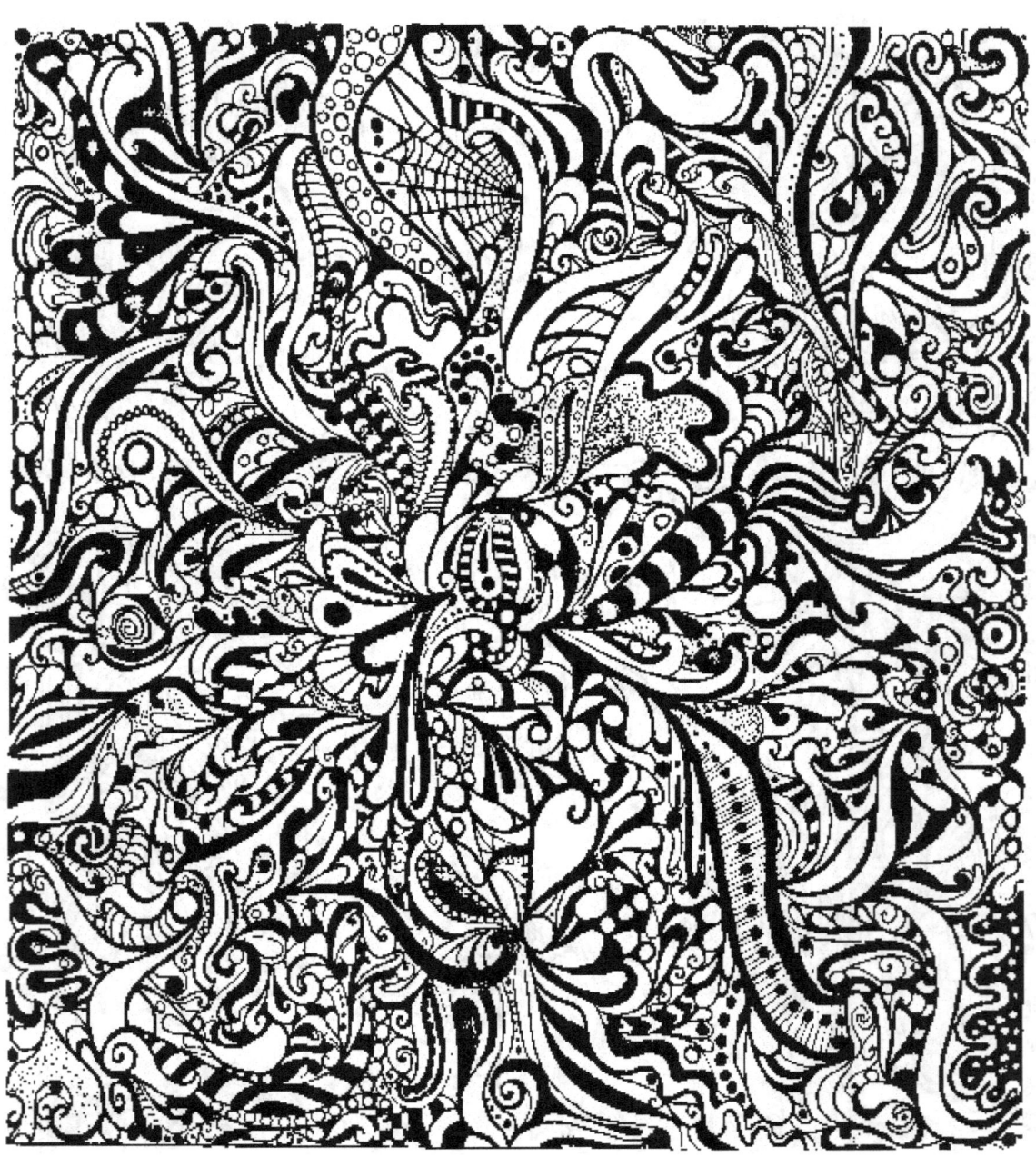

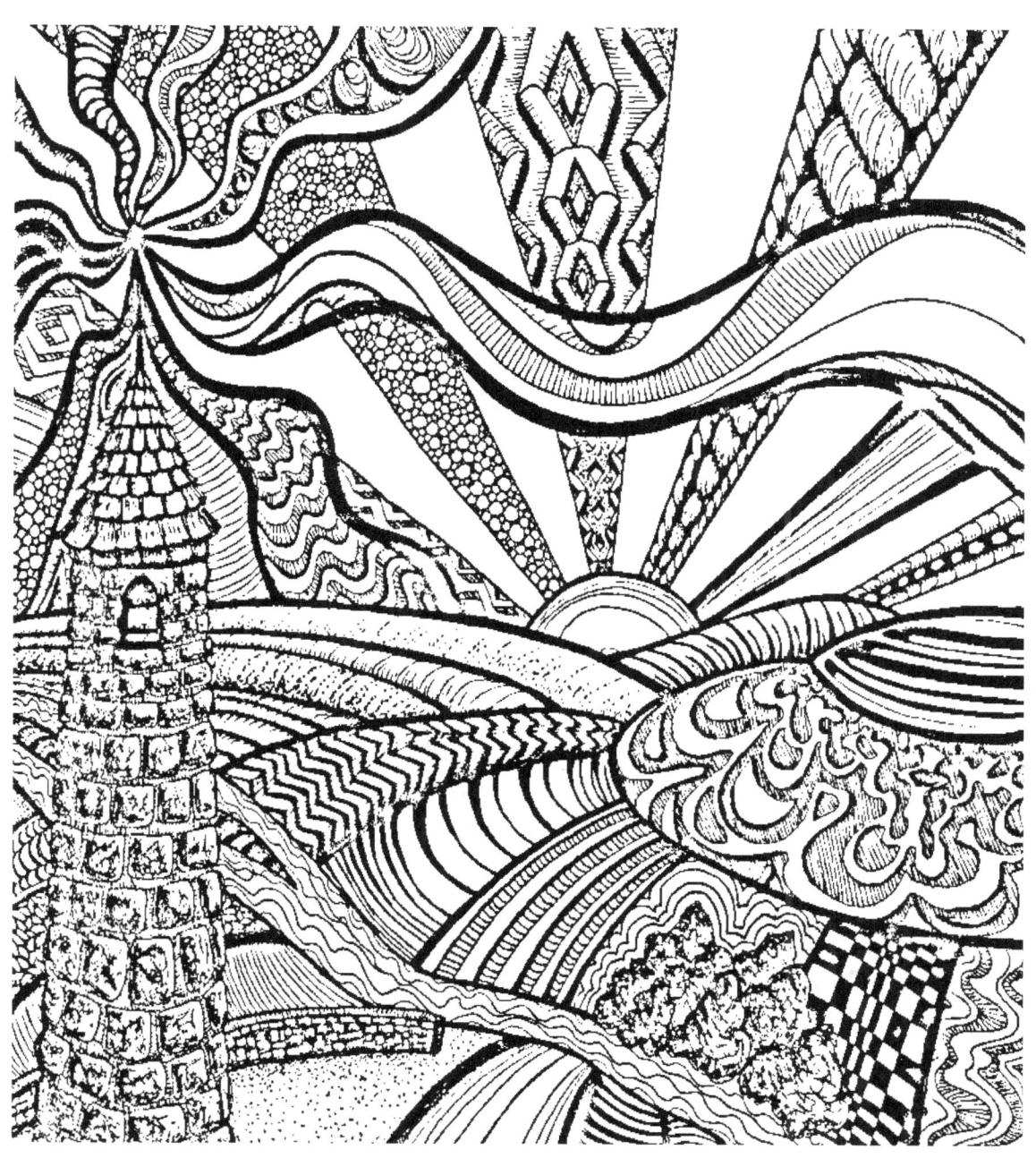

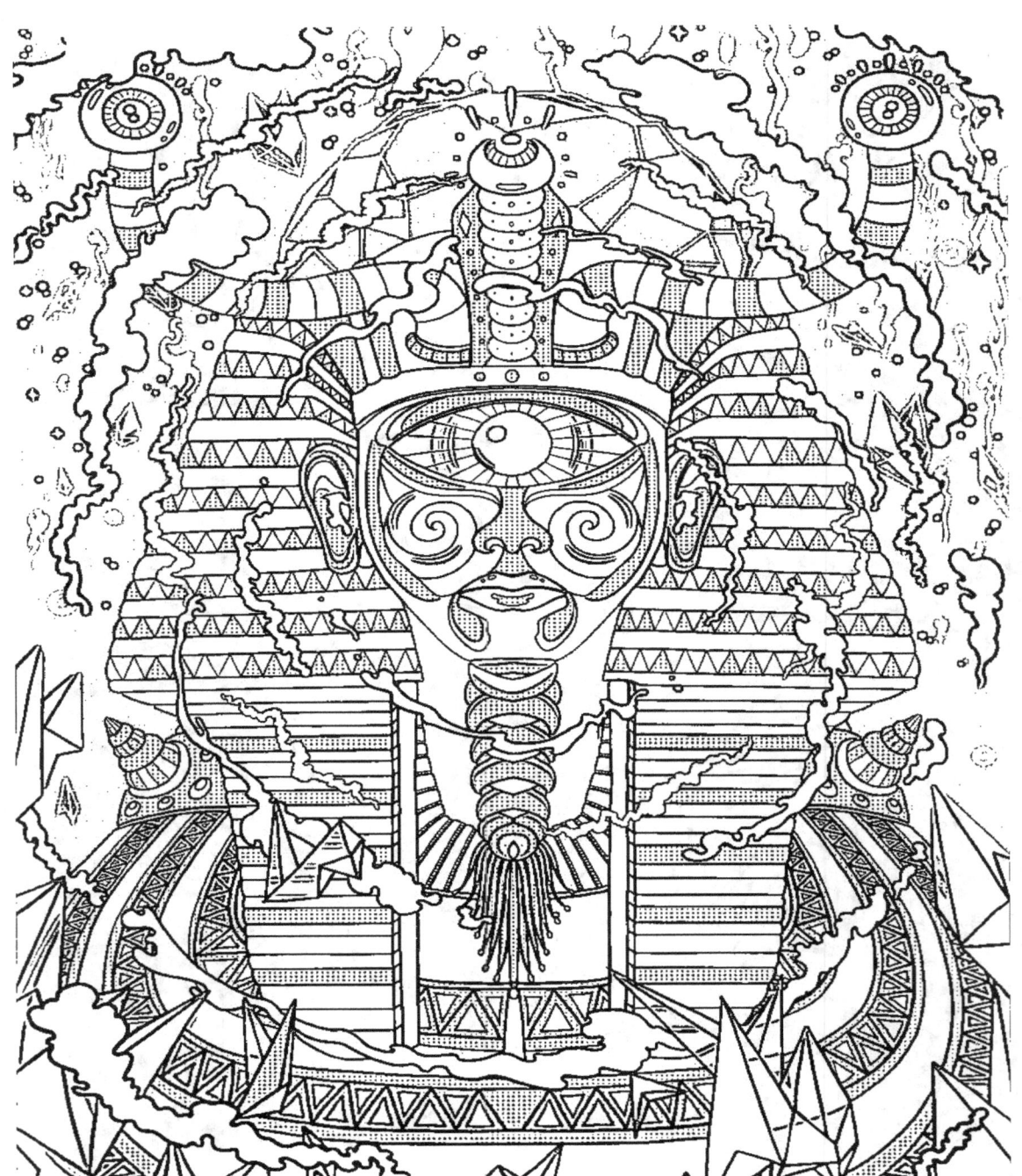

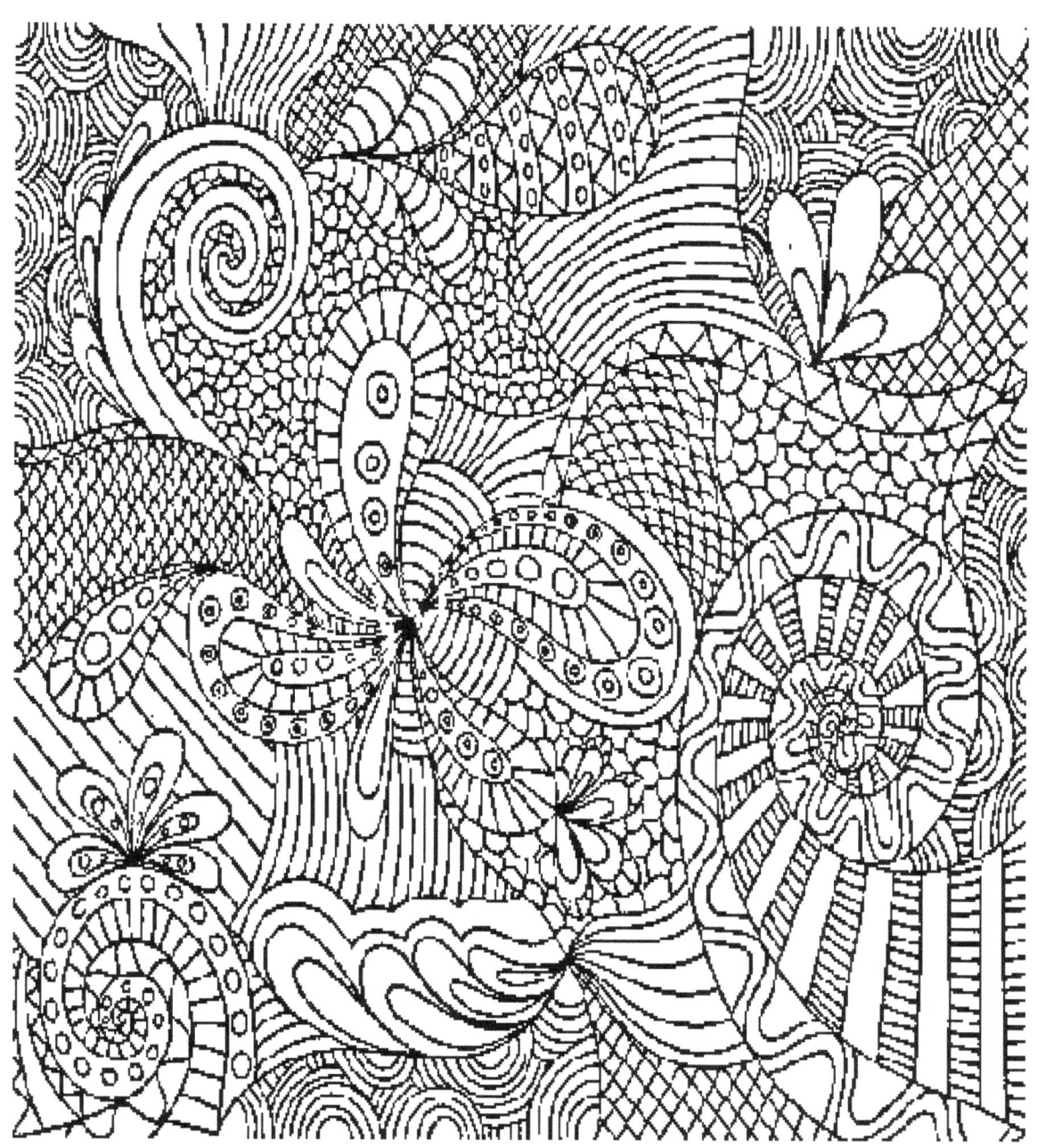

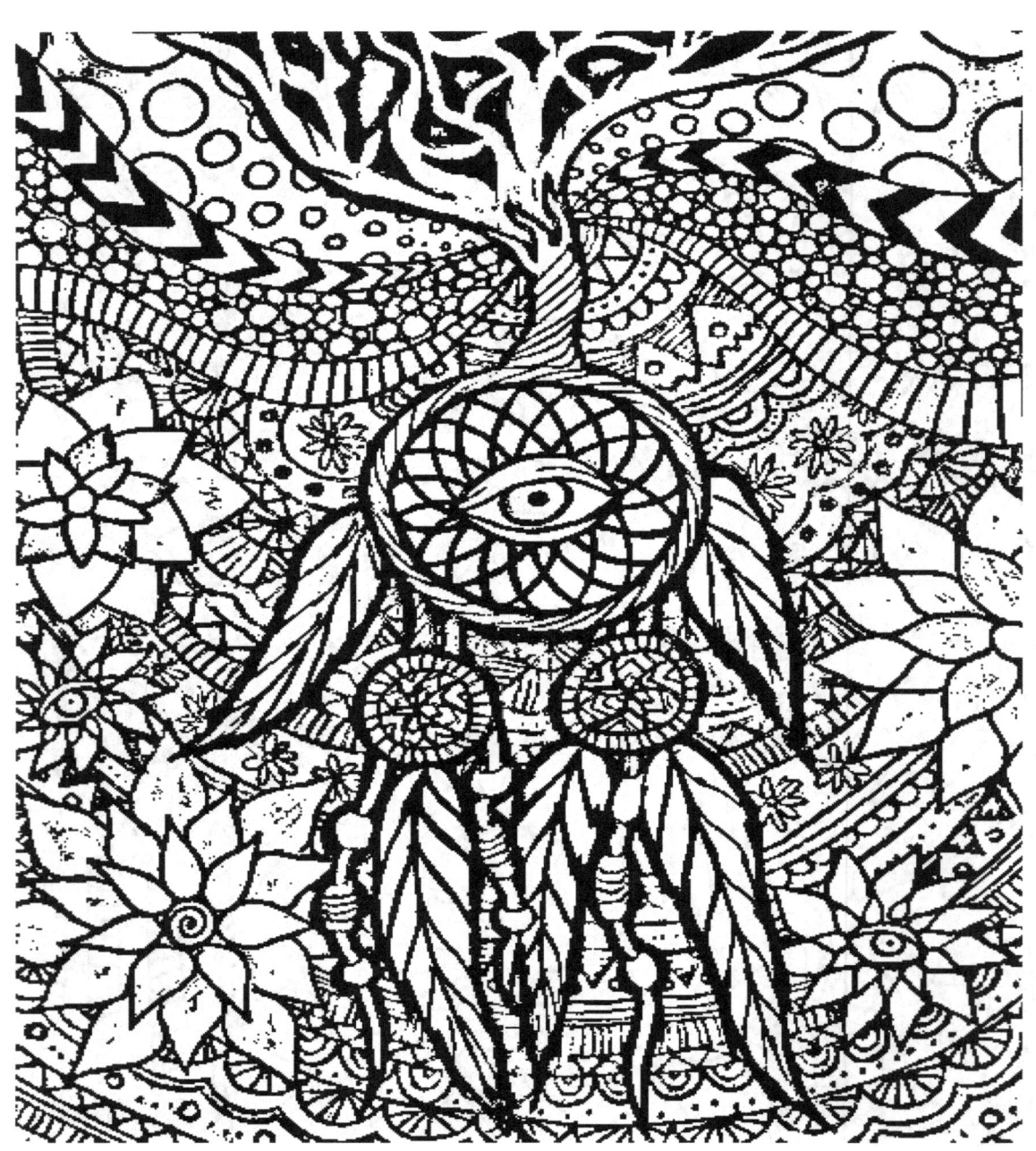

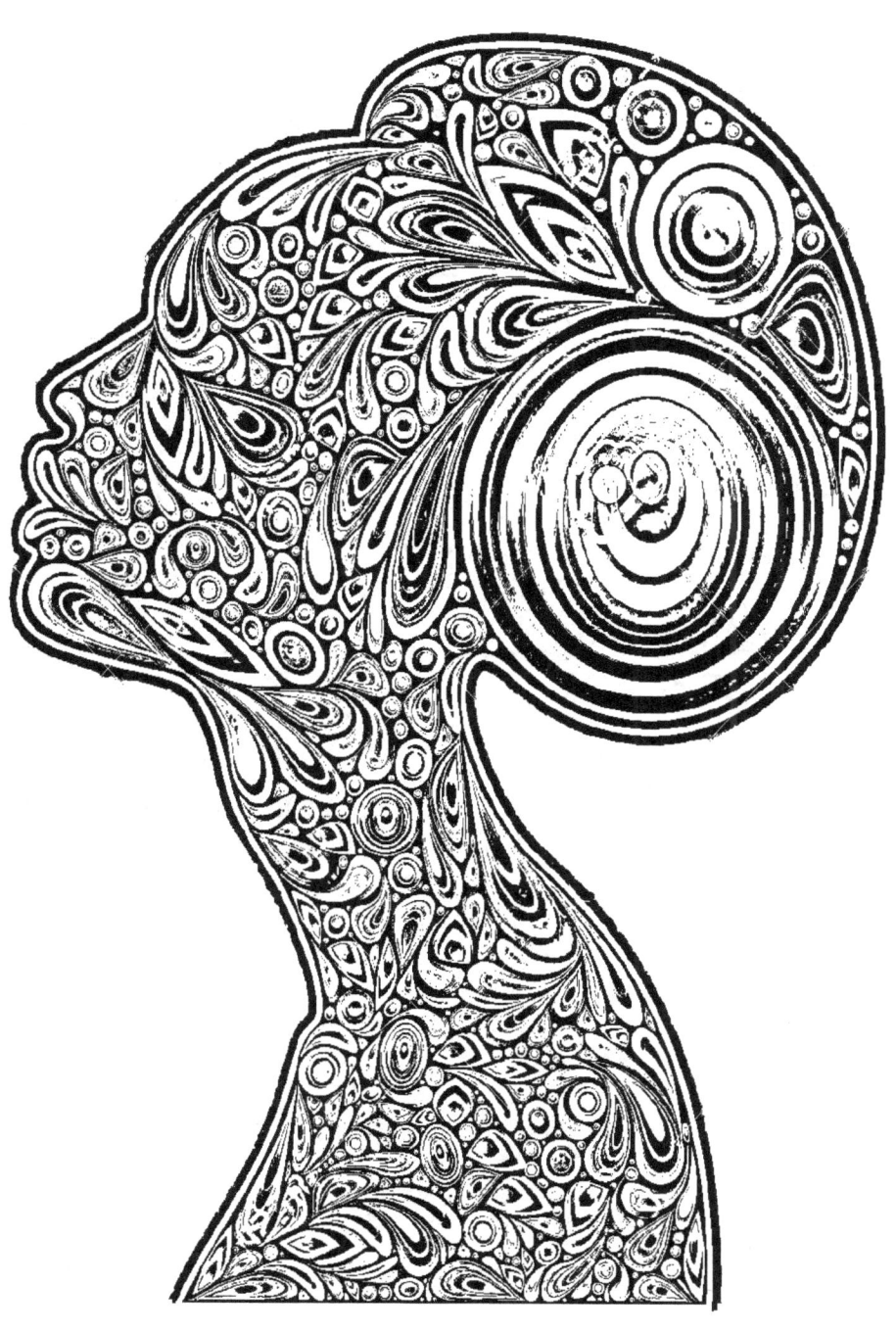

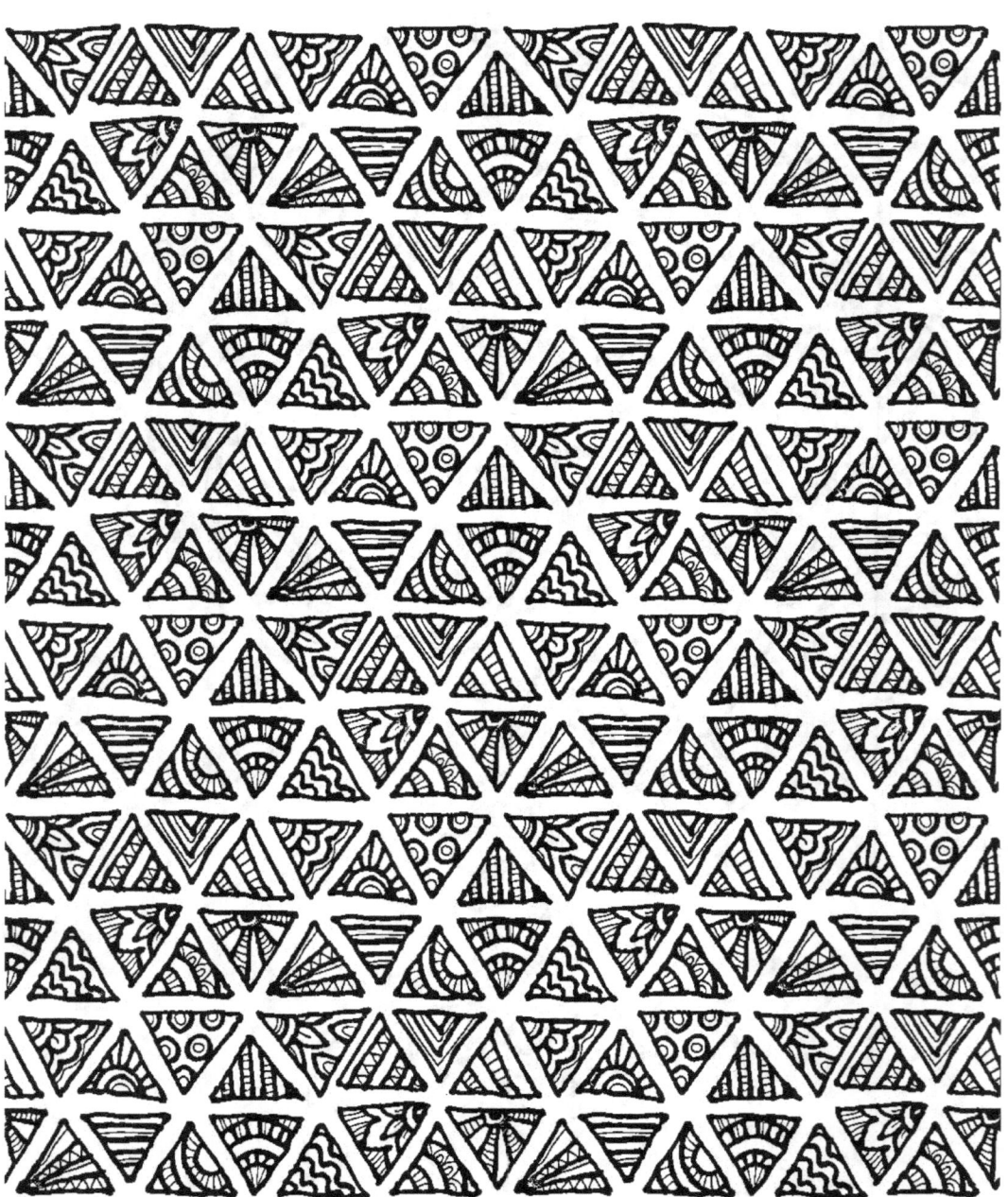

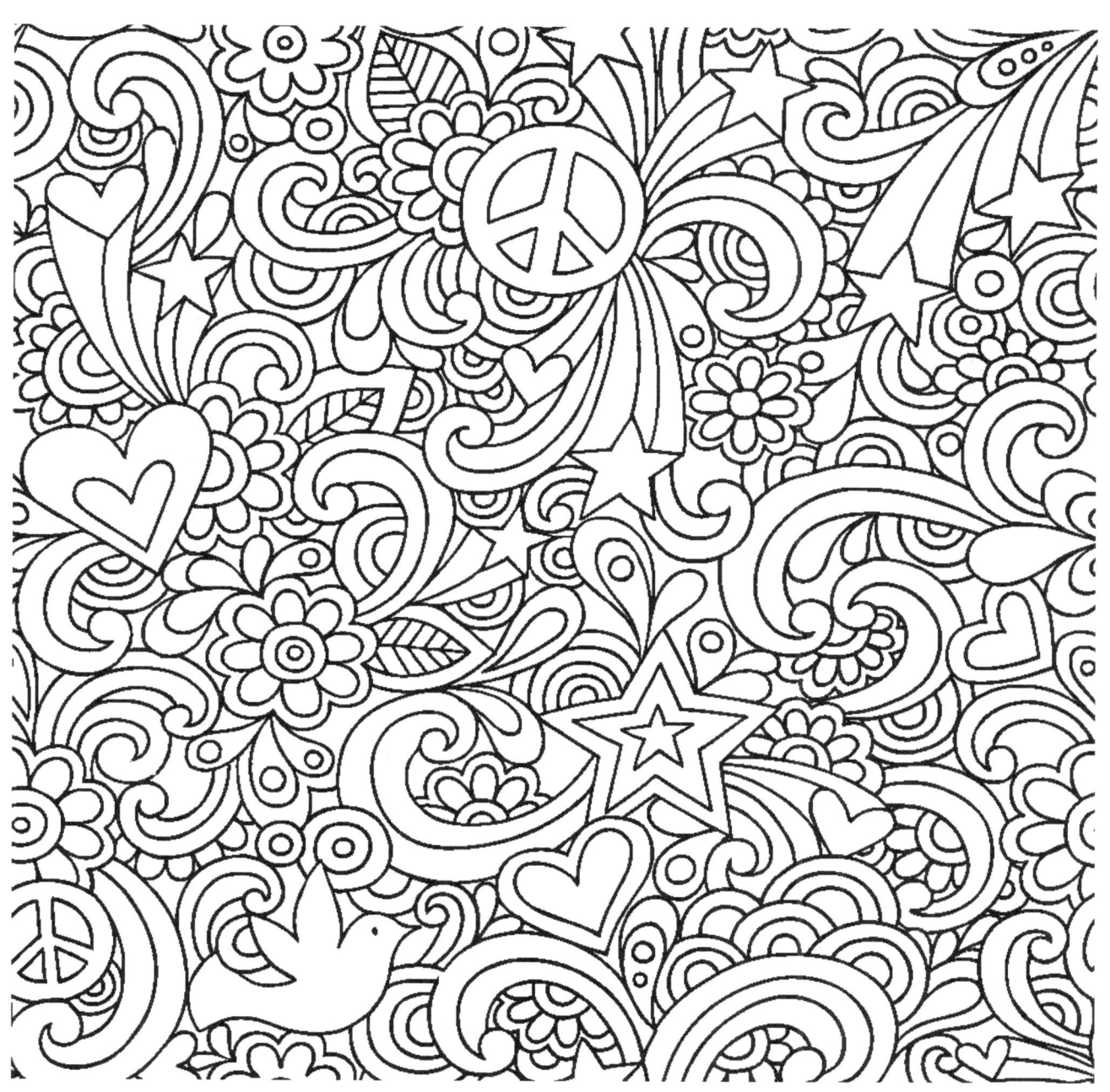

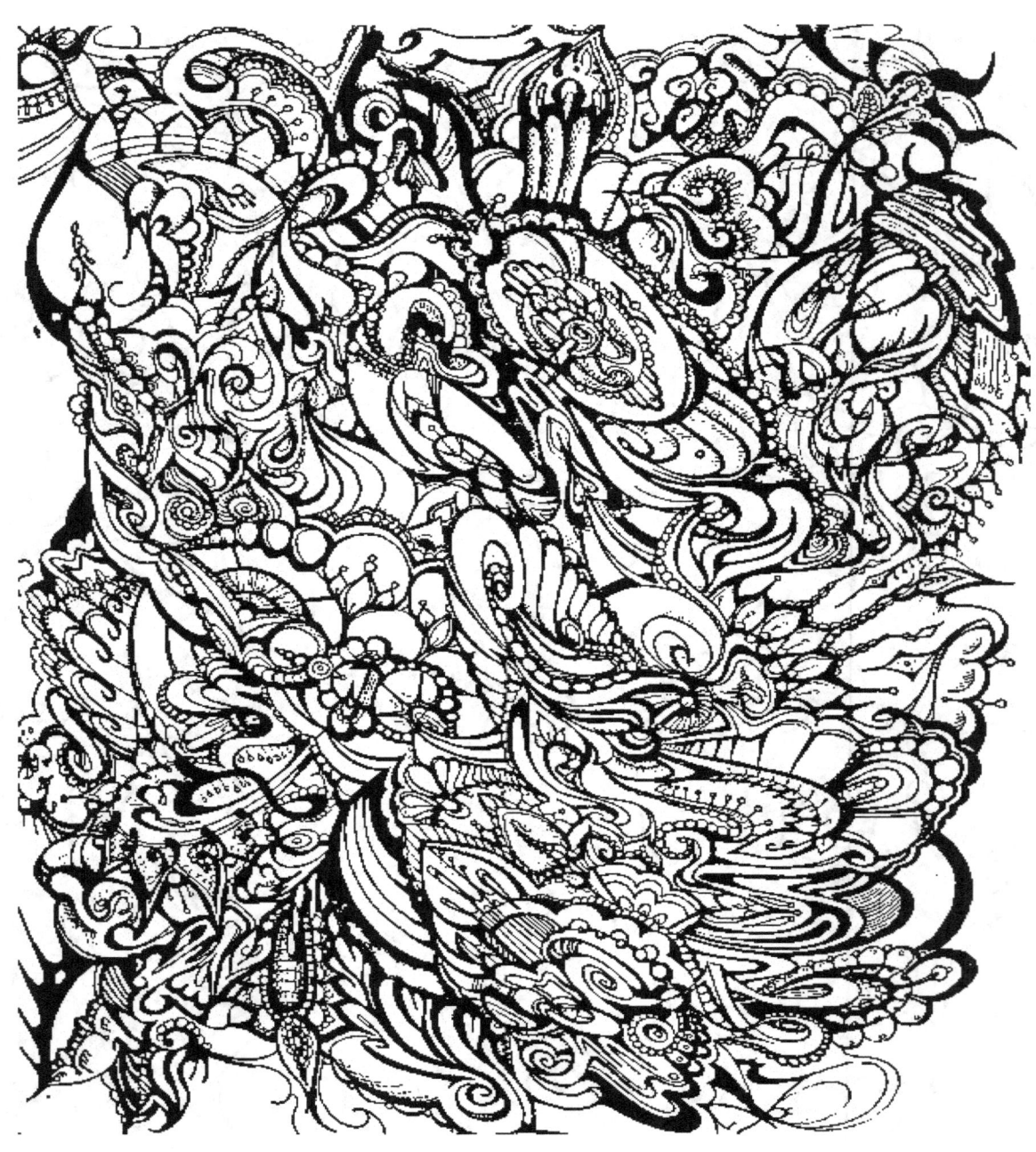

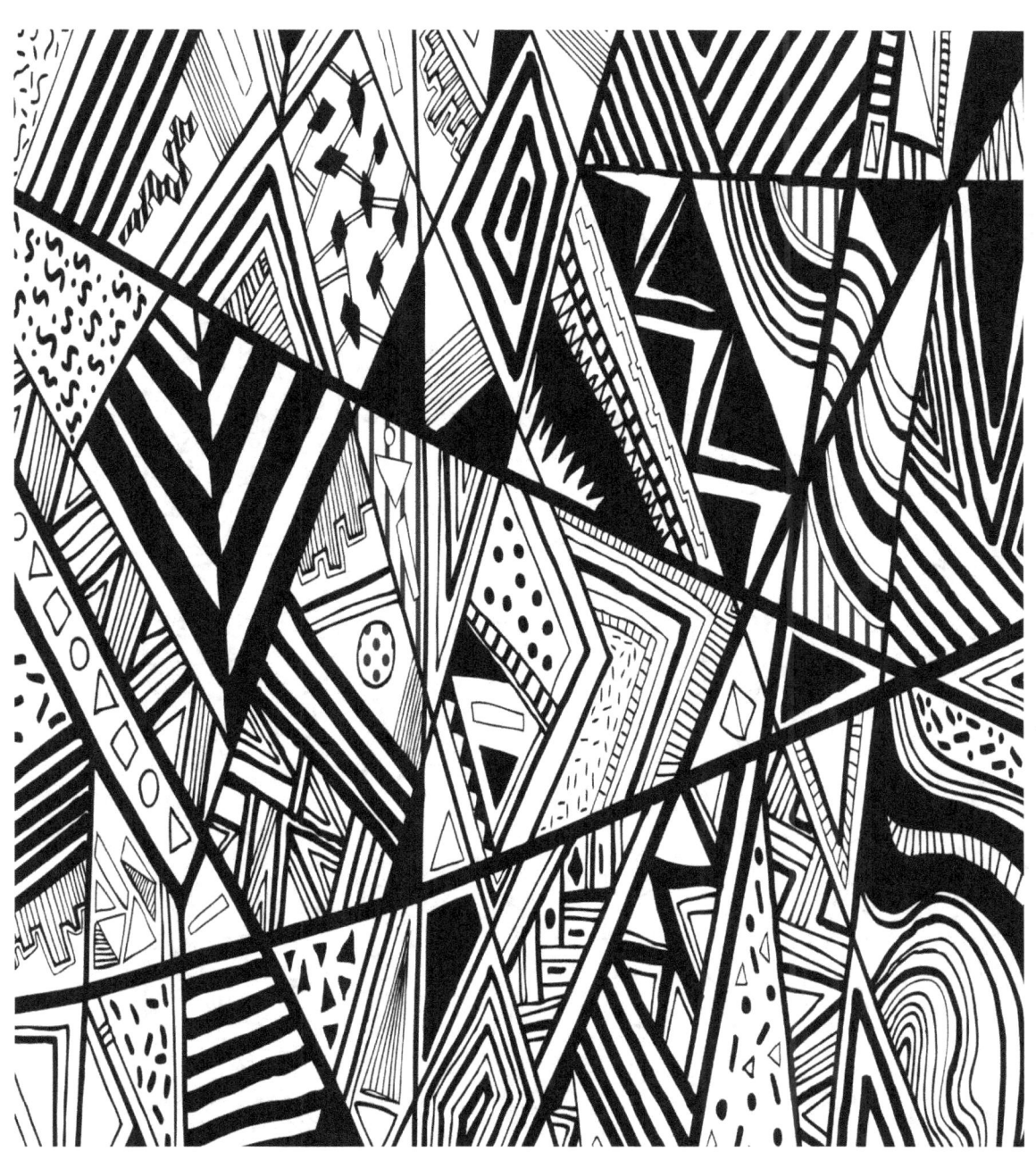

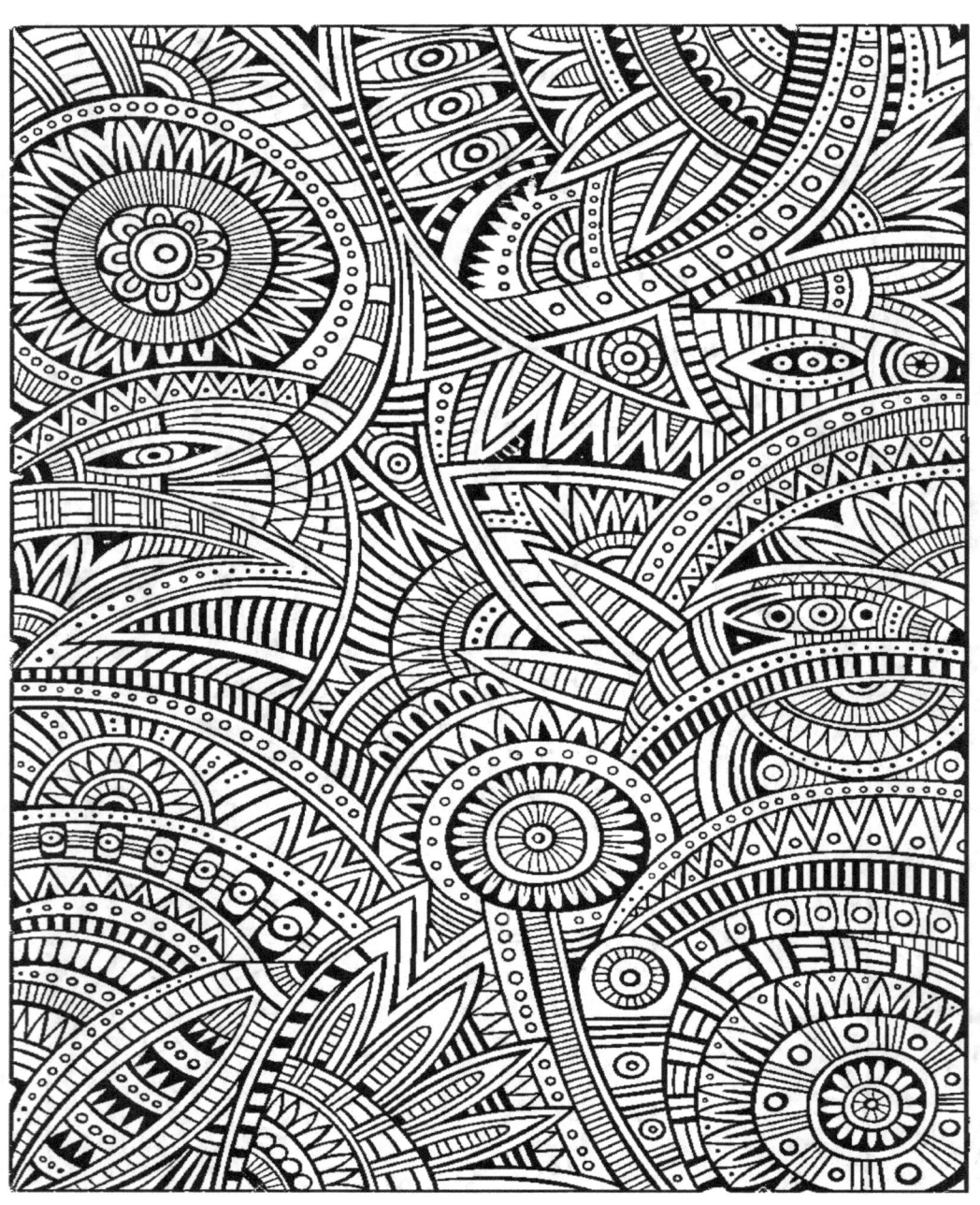

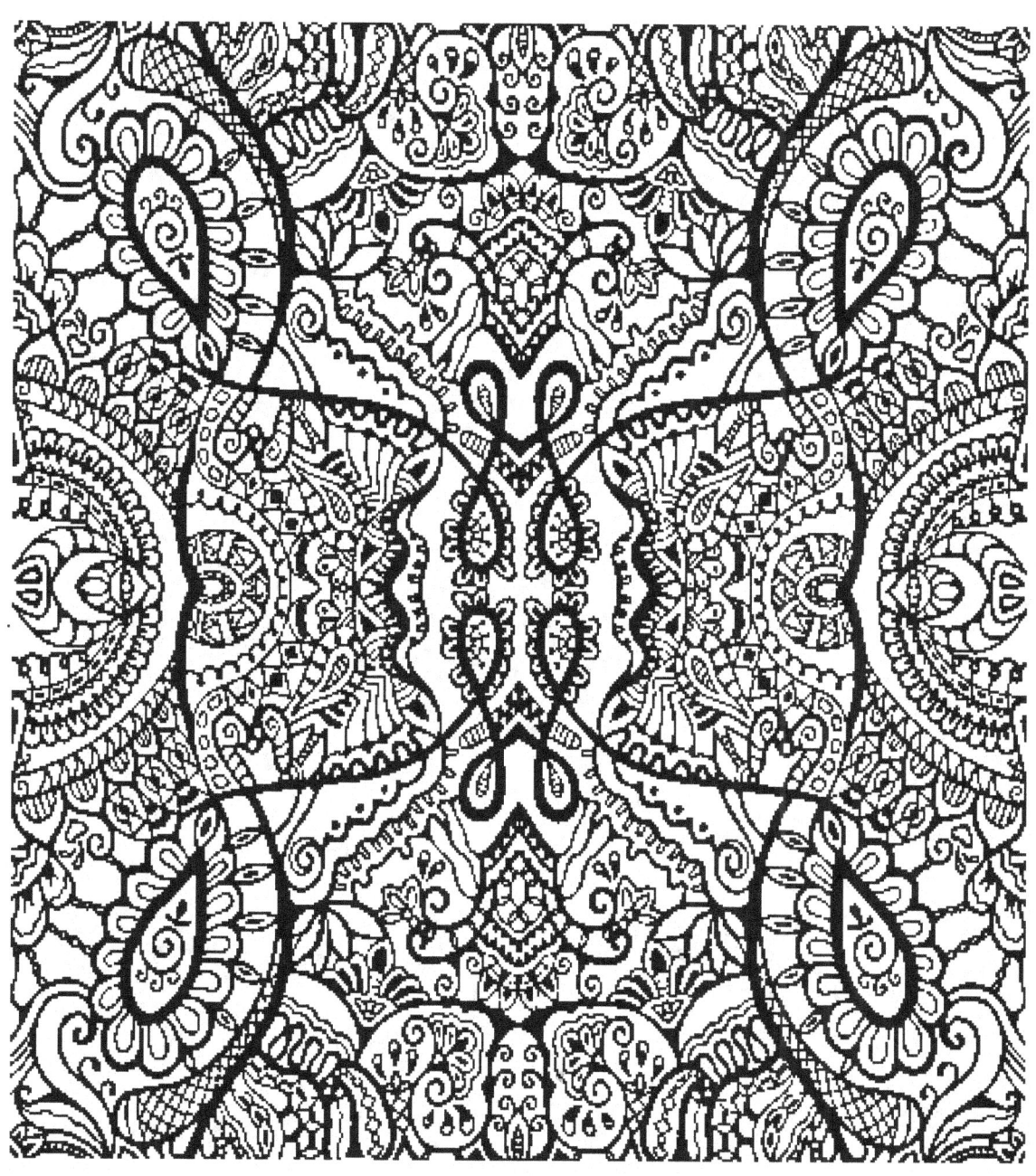

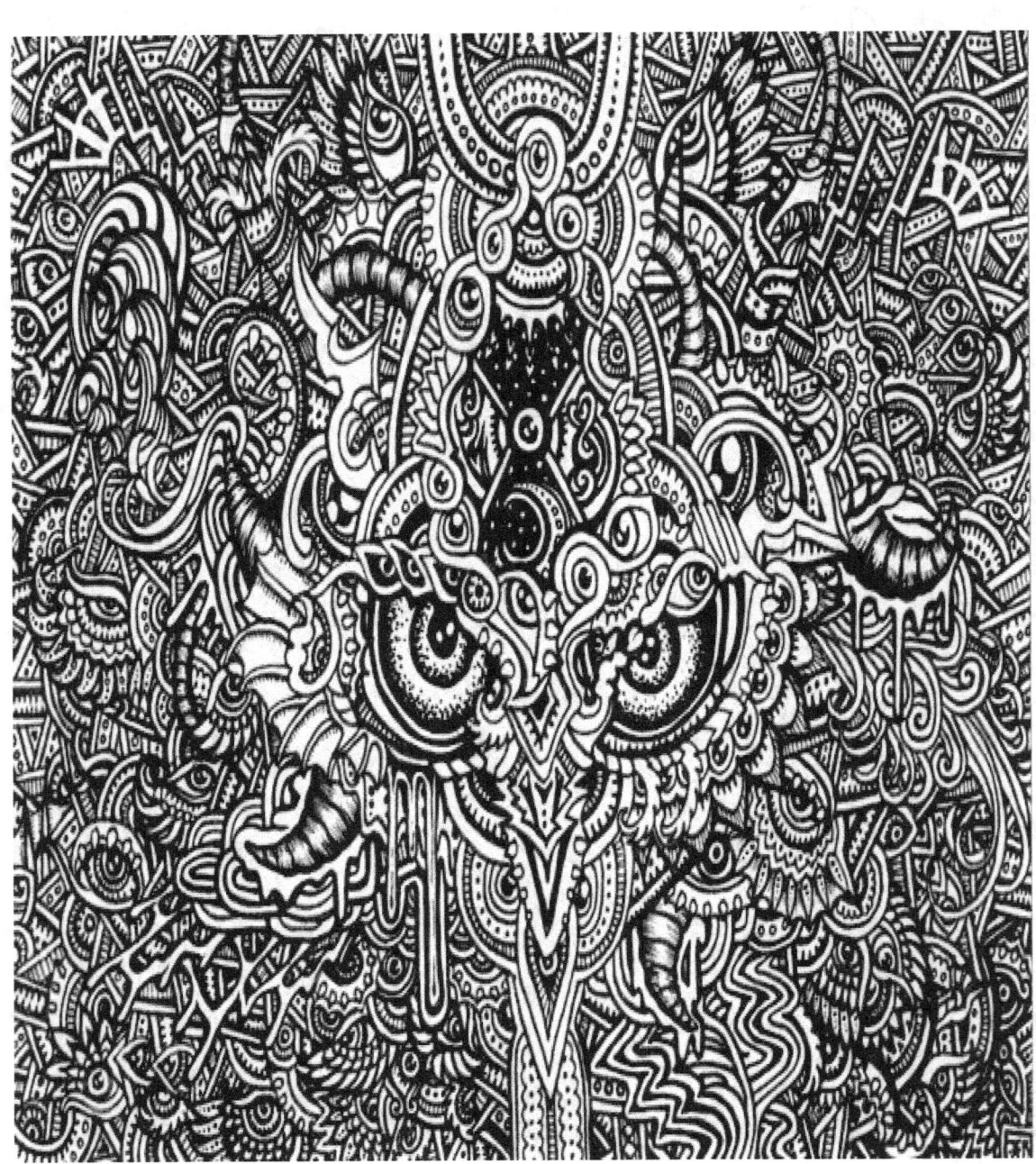

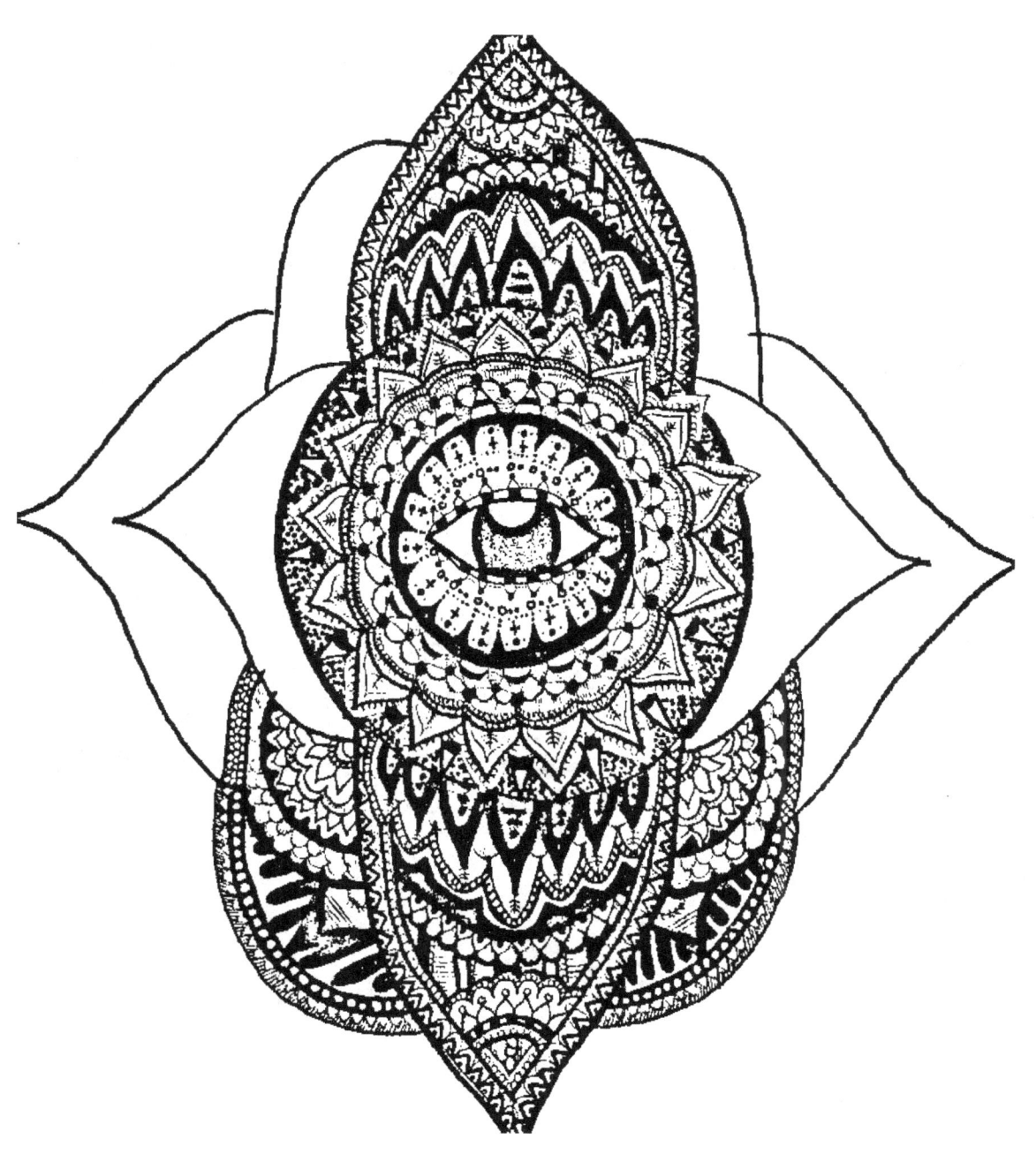

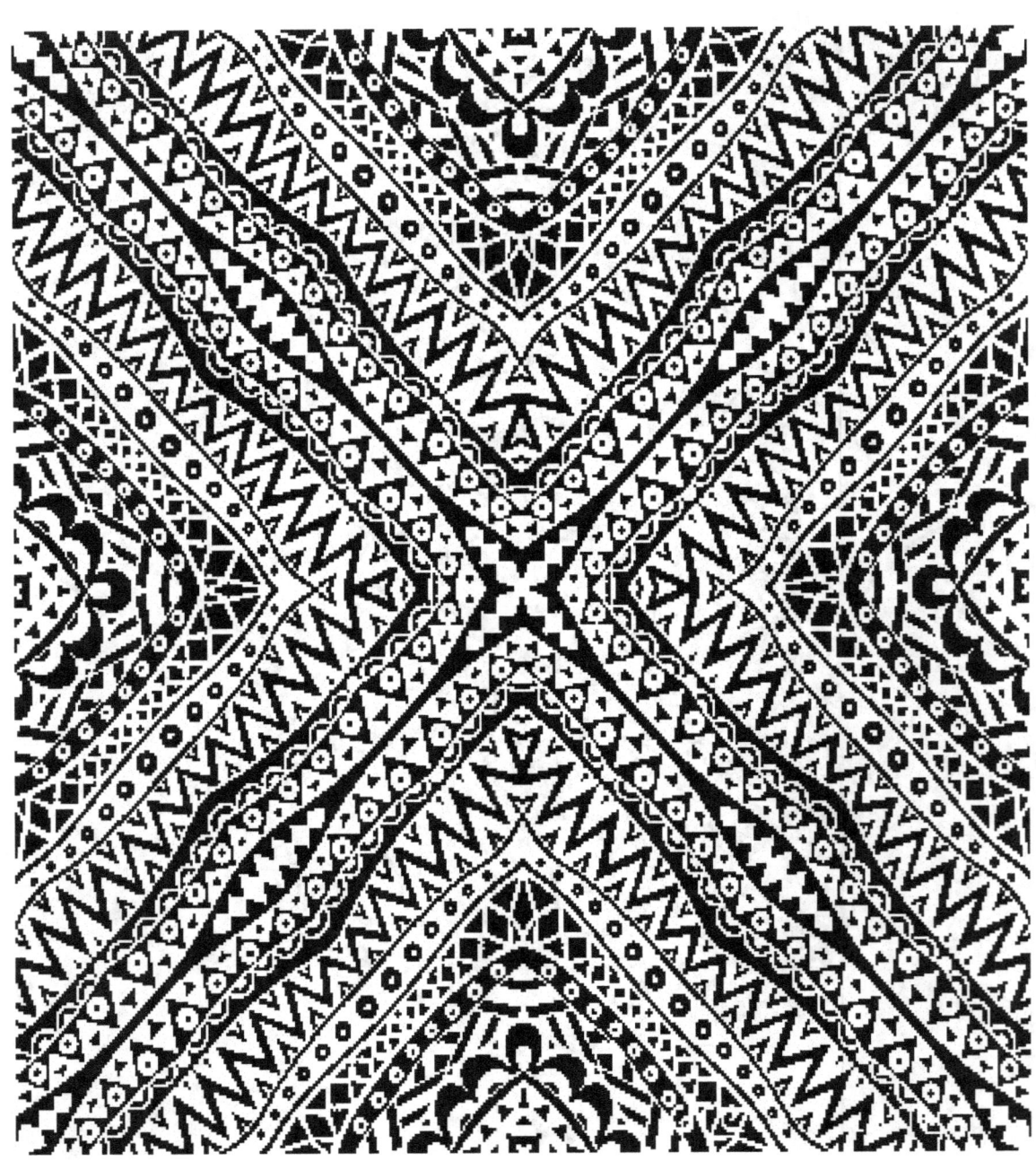

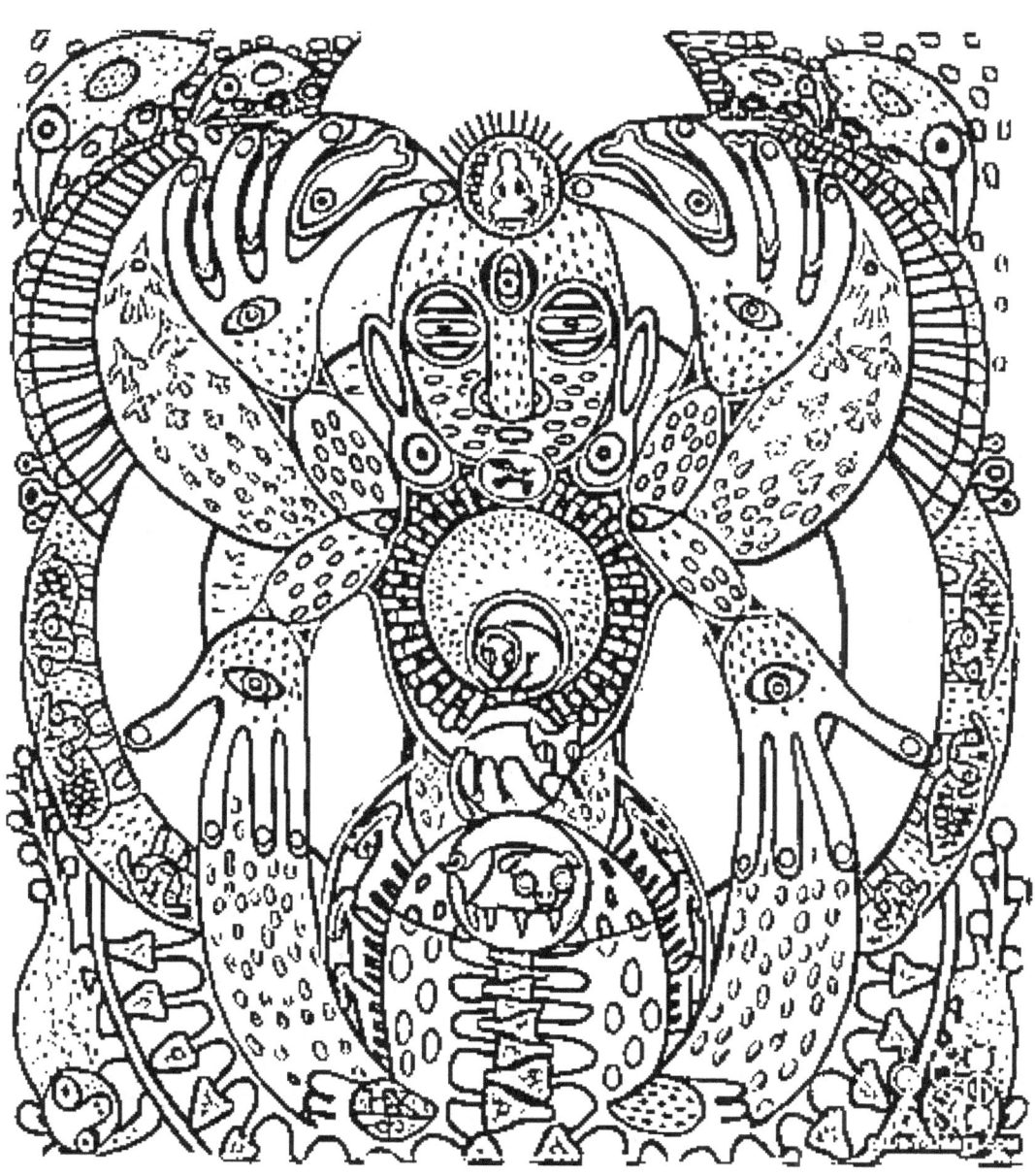

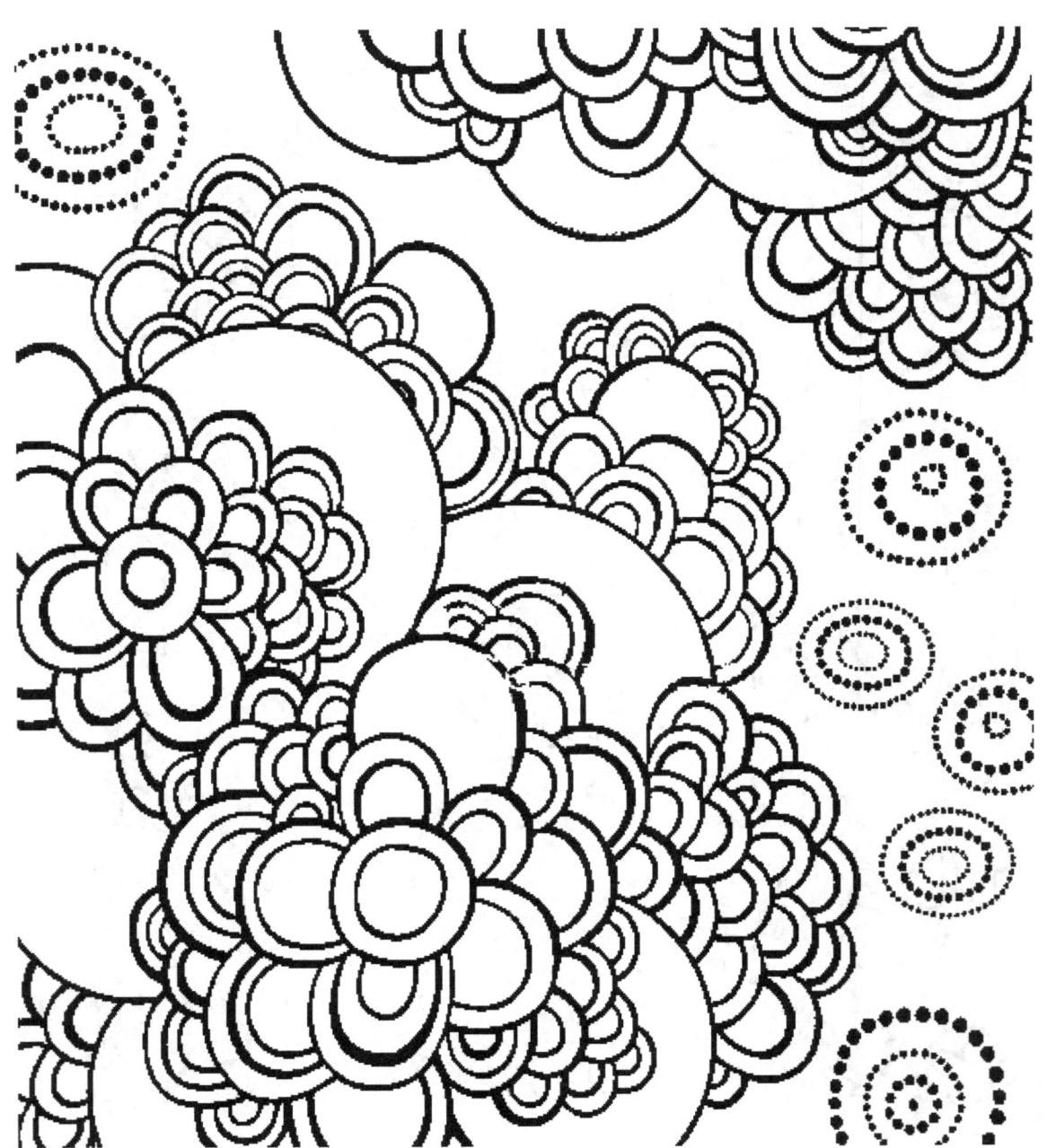

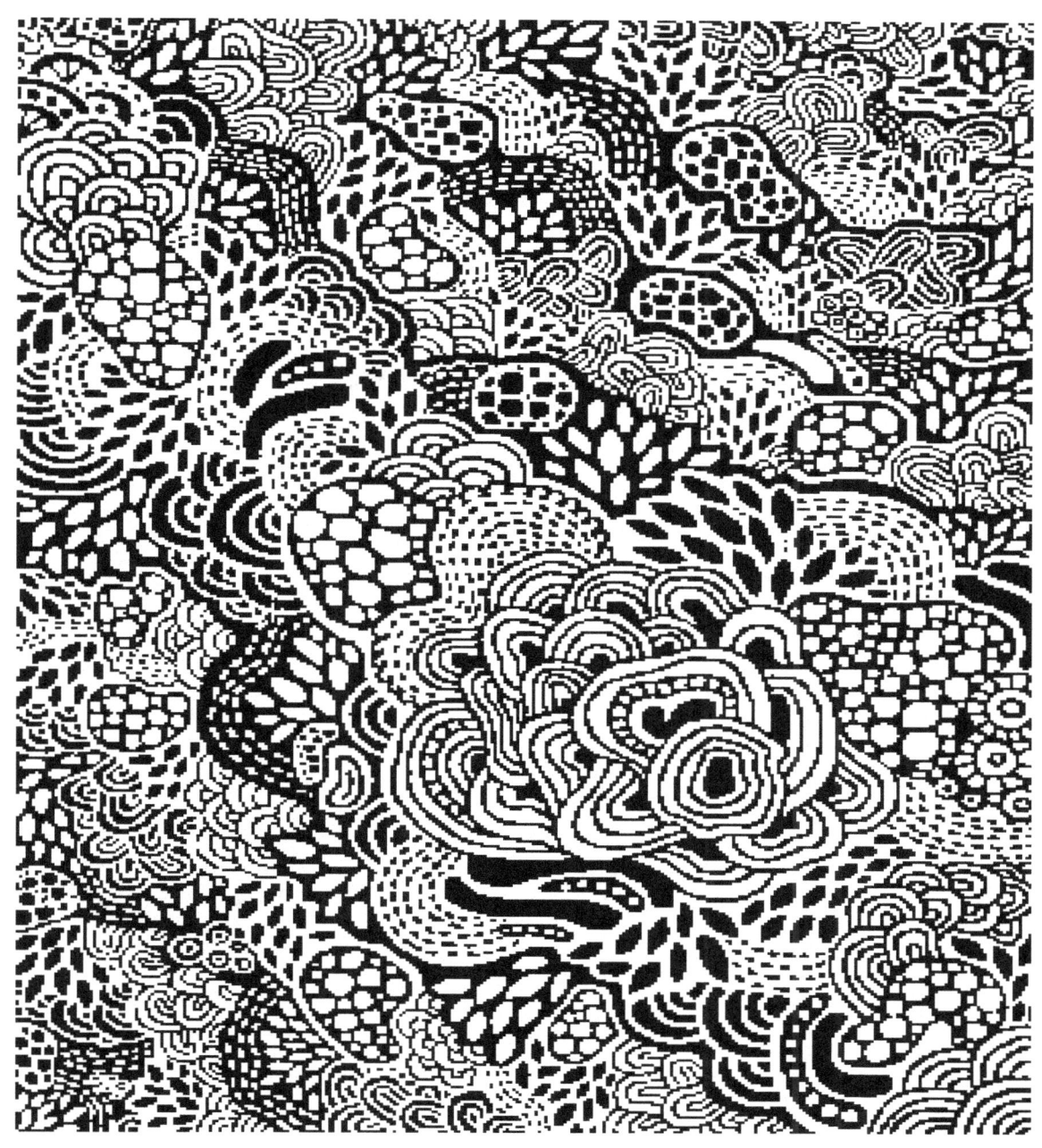